# A Z
## Business
## Studies

## Coursework

# HANDBOOK

Ian Marcousé

3rd edition

## Hodder & Stoughton

A MEMBER OF THE HODDER HEADLINE GROUP

Orders: please contact Bookpoint Ltd, 130 Milton Park, Abingdon, Oxon OX14
4SB. Telephone: (44) 01235 827720, Fax: (44) 01235 400454. Lines are open
from 9.00–6.00, Monday to Saturday, with a 24 hour message answering service.

British Library Cataloguing in Publication Data
A catalogue record for this title is available from the British Library

Hodder Headline's policy is to use papers that are natural, renewable and
recyclable products and made from wood grown in sustainable forests. The logging
and manufacturing processes are expected to conform to the environmental
regulations of the country of origin.

ISBN 0 340 87259 4

First published 1998
Second edition 2001
Third edition 2003

Impression number  10 9 8 7 6 5 4 3
Year                2007 2006 2005 2004

Copyright © 1998, 2001, 2003 Ian Marcousé

Cover photograph: PhotoDisc/Getty Images
Typeset by Phoenix Photosetting, Chatham, Kent
Printed and bound in Great Britain for Hodder & Stoughton Educational,
a division of Hodder Headline, 338 Euston Road, London NW1 3BH
by Cox & Wyman Ltd, Reading, Berks.

# Contents

# Acknowledgements

Many hundreds of students are at the root of this book. Their problems, frustrations and triumphs have been its inspiration. So thanks are due to many past and present students at John Ruskin College, Croydon. More specifically, my daughter Claire has been very helpful, as has the work of: Matthew Evershed, Celia Hugget, Tracey Suckling, Joana D'Souza, Chris Stott, Donna Colucci, Julie Pettit, Julie Hillier, Daniel Collings, Steven Turner, Ali Ramadan and Kamal Kataria. In addition, I would like to acknowledge the amount I have learned about coursework from David Dyer and two of my colleagues at John Ruskin, Roger Raymond and Nigel Watson.

# How to use this book

For this Third Edition I have updated the material and also written new sections for the latest AQA, Edexcel and OCR specifications. Used with care, the First and Second Editions contributed hugely to very high grades for many students. The Third Edition should achieve the same.

The idea for this book came from my own students' struggles with organising their project work. I thought there should be a book as easy to use for coursework as the A–Z Handbook is for looking up business terms. So here it is, The *Complete A–Z Business Studies Coursework Handbook*, written to be the student's personal guide and tutor to a successful project.

Although there are some useful alphabetical sections within the book, the bulk of the text is organised by time. In other words the book starts where a project writer has to start and works through 'titles', 'findings' and 'conclusions' in the same order as the student usually follows. This is to make it as easy as possible to use.

Will anyone read this book from cover to cover? I doubt it. When users of the book want to know how to write up their objectives I expect they will read the relevant section. When they decide to do a feasibility study, they will read that section, and so on. The book will be useful to help set up, research, write up and conclude an assignment. It serves as a permanent tutor/advisor, enabling the student to see where to go next, what to do next and how to maximise marks.

The book is in three parts:

1   a step by step approach through project work, from 'title' to 'objectives', 'method', 'analysis' and finally 'conclusions'

2   an advisory section, explaining in detail about the AQA, Edexcel and Cambridge projects

3   a support section, providing an A–Z of coursework terms and an A–Z of business libraries and other resources.

In addition, there are four project checklists within the book. Each provides an easy way to check on progress at key stages in the project process.

Coursework assessments provide students with a good opportunity to improve their overall A level grades. This book helps to keep projects on track.

*Ian Marcousé*

# Introduction: what is a project/research assignment?

The A Level business studies project is a decision making exercise in the context of an organisational problem or opportunity. The term 'research assignment' means exactly the same. The words 'project' and 'research assignment' will be used interchangeably throughout the book.

The above definition should make it clear that the project is *not* about the past. It should not be a description about how a company solved a problem, or how it grew, or how it coped with change. High grades come from the ability to analyse and evaluate what should be done now or in the future. Inevitably, decisions about what to do require an understanding of the background. Therefore analyses of, for example, past sales or labour turnover figures, may be essential. But looking backwards should only be to help understand the present or future, never for its own sake.

One other key characteristic of a business assignment is that it should be rooted in primary research. The writer must be able to make direct contact with the subject of the project. Reading through textbooks and newspaper articles is not enough. So most projects focus on a local issue, enabling the writer to be able to visit, talk, see and hear.

Must the project be focused on a business? Not necessarily. Charities, hospitals, clubs and schools are all organisations facing a series of management decisions. 'Should Oxfam open a shop in Grantham?' is as valid a project as if the focus was on Tesco.

To the examiner, the research assignment is an opportunity to really see what the student is capable of. Exams are a poor way of assessing initiative, persistence, persuasiveness, presentation or creativity. Projects are excellent at testing all these qualities, so show them! Choose a project that will interest you enough for you to make the extra effort required to excel. Follow the advice in this book and all your efforts will be channelled successfully into writing a better project report. The 15–20% of A level marks represented by the project is within your control. Take advantage of the opportunity to boost your overall grade.

## Projects in Practice 1

Vivien worked at Pizza Hut as a waitress. She decided to look into starting a different type of pizza restaurant. It would offer lighter, Italian-style pizzas and aim at the 18–30 market, rather than families with children. Her manager was willing to provide information about operating costs and profit margins, though she would have to find out the start-up costs for herself. Vivien found out the necessary cost information, and then made an estimate of demand based upon market research and secondary data (such as Pizza Express's annual turnover divided by its number of restaurants). The heart of her project was a fully worked investment appraisal. She concluded that, in Sutton Coldfield, her new pizza restaurant could make £40,000 profit a year – and should be launched.

## Projects in Practice 2

Daniel's father worked at a food distribution company. From its depot in East London (near Millwall Football Club) it supplied over £5 million worth of tinned and packet food to retailers, schools and other major clients throughout Britain. But the business was starting to be stifled, by lack of space and the ever-worsening traffic between the site and the M25 motorway. The student's project looked at the feasibility of moving to a site 12 miles away, close to an M25 junction. What short-term disruption would there be, and how could it be minimised? What would be the financial costs and benefits? How would the move be financed? Did staff acknowledge the need to move? What would be the effect on morale and retention? Daniel was helped to find the answers to all these questions, because the business was keen to find out.

# How to get started

Good projects usually come from four main sources:

1 **business contacts through friends or family**
2 **a part-time job**
3 **a strong school/college link**
4 **your own initiative.**

## 1.1 Business contacts through friends or family

Is anyone in your family a shop owner, a senior manager in a medium-sized company, a club secretary, a company director or a trades union official? All these and many more jobs have the potential to yield a project. Look at the following list of project contact details – all of which have in the past yielded excellent business projects:

| Project contact | Project title |
| --- | --- |
| Family friend is an accountant who has a client in the air-conditioning business | Should BZY Air Conditioning act to reduce its seasonal sales dependence on the summer months? |
| Aunt and uncle run a dry-cleaning business | Should a dry-cleaners diversify to offer a 'take and deliver' service to local businesses? |
| Mother is human resources manager at a large mobile phone company | Should Aircall plc change or scrap its performance related pay scheme? |
| Father runs an off-licence | How can the loss-making BJP off-licence be returned to breakeven and then profitability? |

If set up correctly, personal contacts with family or friends have huge potential. Projects require a lot of time and effort from the contacts. They will need to explain business procedures, help to gather and explain data, answer queries and help to fill knowledge gaps. There may also be a requirement to spend some money, travel or on postage when carrying out a postal survey. Strong personal contacts are much more likely to help by getting the contact company to pay up.

However, as the table below shows, there are disadvantages as well as advantages to using family or friends:

| Advantages of projects with family/friends | Disadvantages of projects with family/friends |
|---|---|
| ✓ They are more likely to make an effort to help you | ✗ but they may underestimate you ('Little Jimmy! Gosh you've grown!') |
| ✓ They may be willing to bend rules to help you get semi-confidential data | ✗ but may provide everything at arms' length, with you never visiting the workplace, just getting documents brought home (fathers can be especially guilty of this). |
| ✓ It is more likely that daily access will be provided, instead of a one-off week at a firm | ✗ but unlimited access may mean that it's never quite the right day to start serious work. |
| ✓ Market research can be expensive, especially if questionnaires need to be posted; family/friends are more likely to help. | |

### Projects in Practice

Jacqui's mother knew a young couple who opened a print company called BCS. Jacqui knew both people, though not especially well. Fortunately, when she visited the business she found them friendly and helpful. The company had expanded to turn over £250,000 a year and employ seven staff. Now the company had the opportunity to win a large, new order worth £150,000 per year for each of the next three years. What would be the physical, personnel and financial implications? Should the order be accepted?

> **Continued**
>
> Jacqui looked into the costs of moving premises (which she thought essential) and of buying extra printing machinery. She eventually recommended that the profit margins on the order did not merit the upheaval involved.

If you are certain that you want to use a family/friend/contact, you should now turn to page 11 to see how to develop it.

## 1.2 A part-time job

You may be working at a supermarket checkout, a McDonalds drive-thru window or a pet shop. Wherever you work, your employer faces business problems or opportunities. As long as your boss is willing to co-operate, you have a business project at your fingertips. Look carefully at the following list. On the left are student jobs and on the right are the assignment titles those students came up with.

| Student's job | Project title |
| --- | --- |
| Saturday job at Eisenegger (clothes shop) | Should Eisenegger change the discount pricing policy they currently use? |
| Evening/weekend job at Burger King | A study into the feasibility of opening up a new Burger King outlet in Waddon. |
| Saturday job at a butcher's shop | A study into how a small, independent butcher could survive (or even thrive) in a declining market. |
| Evening/weekend job at Safeway deli counter | Should the Croydon Safeway deli double the space it devotes to selling hot food? |
| Working at a Dillons Newsagents | How could the profitability of the XXX branch be improved to match that at Dillon's best performing branch, and thereby ensure its survival? |

The great strength of an assignment based upon a part-time job is that you are already there, on a regular basis, so you keep picking up extra titbits of information with which to build up your project. Yet there are disadvantages as well, as shown in the following table.

| Advantages of projects based on a part-time job | Disadvantages of projects based on a part-time job |
|---|---|
| ☑ You have some background understanding of how the organisation works | ☒ though you may think your knowledge is better than it really is; make sure to gain a full understanding of the managerial viewpoint. |
| ☑ You are there every week, so the project can develop steadily | ☒ … but this can make you feel trapped in a job where you are unhappy. (This happened to the student in the butcher's shop mentioned above.) |
| ☑ Consistent interest shown by the student often yields data that is usually treated as highly confidential. | ☒ … though when working at multiple outlets such as Sainsbury's or McDonald's, head office rules may mean figures are never made available. |
| ☑ If a manager is interested in the project s/he may be willing to help with photocopying and by allowing interviews with staff or customers | ☒ … but managers come and go, so a project may start off being well supported, but go downhill when a new manager arrives. |
| ☑ Inside knowledge of morale and motivation on the shop floor is useful. | ☒ … but students can end up writing reports which are long whinges about staff (i.e. themselves) being undervalued and underpaid. |

If you are certain that you want to base your research assignment on your part-time job turn to page 11 to see how to develop it.

### Projects in Practice

Joana worked at Makro, the large cash and carry wholesaler. Her boss agreed to let her carry out a project, and even to help with it. The topic was to be the store's new management information system, (the computer system governing stock ordering, deliveries, work scheduling and management accounts). Joana was to make recommendations on how the system could be improved. This was a major task, requiring interviews with managers and supervisors in various Makro stores. The business proved quite helpful with what was a very demanding project. The nature of the task meant that Joana learned an enormous amount about the management style and attitudes within the business. This enriched her classroom understanding and motivation towards the subject as a whole. Her project obtained a grade B.

## 1.3 A strong school/college link

Some schools and colleges have excellent contacts with local firms. Work experience, factory visits and visiting speakers may all be focused upon one or two local companies. It is natural, therefore, that you may be given the opportunity of researching a project based upon the same firm or firms. This approach is attractive because you know that the firm is committed to helping; you are not reliant upon one manager's whim. Yet there are some major disadvantages to a school/college link, as follows:

**Pros of working with a strong school/college link**

☑ Your teacher is likely to know a lot about the firm, perhaps including good contacts

☑ If the school/college link is well established at a senior level, junior managers may provide good access to semi-confidential data

**Cons of working with a strong school/college link**

☒ ... but beware of assuming that knowledge exists; contact may be limited to placings for work experience, which is far less demanding than project research.

☒ ... but links through careers teachers or Young Enterprise can prove insufficiently deep to sustain a good project.

☑ A supportive firm is likely to be generous with resources such as photocopying facilities

☒ … though the fact that the firm is supportive may restrict you from asking and writing critically or even objectively.

As with any project contact, it is important to make an early visit. Be clear from the start about what your contact is expecting. Has your careers teacher implied that little more is needed than a week's work experience? Or is the firm clear that good projects require good data and searching questions? The very fact that the link is through your school/college may make you think 'Oh, it'll be all right'. Don't fall into this trap! Check first by visiting and talking things over (in line with the advice given in Chapter 3). If your contact is as helpful as your school/college hopes, you may be able to come up with project titles such as the following:

| Contact with local organisation | Resulting project title |
| --- | --- |
| Personnel department of a branch of Marks & Spencer. | A comparison between induction procedures at the Marks & Spencer and BhS branches in Coventry, to identify ways M&S could improve. |
| Production department of a major frozen food producer. | A study into whether a new, £400,000 production unit for pizza toppings would be financially worthwhile. |
| Distribution section of a soft drinks producer. | Should a new fleet of lorries be purchased or leased? |
| Recruitment section of the local police force. | Can the XXX police force overcome its recruitment shortfall by better use of its existing budget or must a bigger budget be allocated? |

If you are certain that you want to make use of school/college links for your project, turn to page 11 to see how to develop it.

## 1.4 Your own initiative

This seems the most difficult way to tackle a business project, yet many are very successful. This is partly, perhaps, because you know from the start that the project is all down to you. Others have the excuse of waiting for someone to provide information, but approached in this way you simply have to keep on going. But what would you do and how would you do it? Almost certainly you will need to carry out a feasibility study into setting up a business of your own choice. One method of approaching this is set out in Chapter 16. For now it is worth noting that, at schools/colleges experienced with business projects, as many as half the candidates complete feasibility studies on their own initiative. They start with no business contacts at all. The method has disadvantages as well as advantages:

| Advantages of projects based on own initiative | Disadvantages of relying on own initiative |
|---|---|
| ☑ The project is the student's idea (or even ambition) which may help motivation | ☒ … though if the focus is a really wacky idea, there may be no secondary data available. |
| ☑ The initiative required to obtain data impresses the examiner | ☒ … but getting data can be very difficult for those without access to a good library and for those who are shy. |
| ☑ Feasibility studies require a great detail of numerical analysis, therefore they tend to generate good marks | ☒ … the highest marks, though, more commonly come from projects based on a contact within a company. |
| ☑ You are not reliant upon the continued goodwill of a contact at a firm | ☒ … but you lose the opportunity to learn the methods and attitudes within a real business. |

In reality, the students most likely to rely on their own initiative are those with no choice. They have no viable contacts. But this apparent disadvantage may be no such thing. Students with contacts start confidently, even smugly. Those without feel vulnerable. By the end of the project process the situation can be reversed. This book sets out clearly how to carry out a feasibility study. So the problem of deciding how to carry out the project is reduced.

The table on the next page gives some ideas of coursework titles and how they came about.

| Origins of the project idea | Project title |
|---|---|
| This student thought it time to combine Indian food with the speed and style of McDonald's. | Is it feasible to start up an Indian fast food outlet in Luton? |
| Problems with organising driving lessons led to an idea for basing the sales office on site. | A study of the viability of a new driving school based at John Leggott College, Scunthorpe. |
| A student doing an Art and Design course thought there was a gap in the market she could fill. | A feasibility study into setting up an art materials shop in Selsdon. |
| A morning spent queuing for tennis tickets convinced one student that a lot of money could be made from specially designed T-shirts. | Would it be profitable to start up a business producing and selling T-shirts aimed at special events such as Wimbledon and the FA Cup Final? |

## Projects in Practice

David's assignment went wrong. It had been arranged with his boss at work, but changes in personnel made it impossible to obtain the figures he needed. So he switched, late on, to conduct 'a feasibility study into positioning a new J. Sainsbury supermarket'. With no contacts within Sainsbury's, David's only sources of information were: Sainsbury's annual accounts, market intelligence information, primary research among shoppers at the local Safeway and Tesco, and an analysis of local traffic flows and transport links.

The annual accounts enabled him to identify a number of key points. The property valuation (£3538 million) divided by the number of stores (355) implied a property cost per store of £9.97 million. Similar calculations provided useful pointers to stock requirements, fixtures and fittings and labour costs. David was able to produce a worthwhile project in just under five weeks, gaining a grade C.

# 1.5 Other sources of projects

It is risky to generalise, but some starting points for projects often lead to poor results. These include:

a **Young Enterprise.** Although a very worthwhile introduction to business courses, Young Enterprise is rarely a good starting point for a research assignment. It is designed to be a short-lived, fun activity, not a carefully researched, academic exercise.

b **GCSE projects.** You may well have produced excellent GCSE coursework, but it is a mistake to assume that A level projects merely have a higher word count. The key difference between the two is the degree of academic rigour. It is easy to make a piece of work longer, but very hard to make it more rigorous. To quote the classic answer when asked for directions, 'I wouldn't start from here'.

c **Work experience.** It may be that a genuine project idea stems from work experience. But it is not realistic to think that a week's work experience represents the research element of a project. If you are to undertake work experience, try to visit your contact beforehand, to discuss the possibility of undertaking a project. Then, perhaps, the work experience can be tailored to your project needs.

d **A factory visit.** If you are studying in a rural area, it may seem that a factory visit is the best way of providing the material for a project. In reality, you cannot expect to get sufficient data for tackling any business problem from one visit. If your goal is a good grade, think harder about your local area. Farming is a business, so are fishing and tourism. Business opportunities exist everywhere, so relying on a factory visit is unnecessary.

Far more promising than the above are opportunities arising from your own life. The clubs you belong to, the sporting or social activities you enjoy and so on. As long as you have good, willing contacts a project can be based on these activities, as in the following example.

## Projects in Practice

Chris was a keen diver and an active member of the British Sub-Aqua Club (BSAC). His local branch was facing financial difficulties due to a drop in membership. This decline was leading to 'a vicious circle ... fixed overheads

**Continued**

must still be met and the club has been forced through the loss of members to raise its subscription fees from £70 to £140 in two years.' The local and national club officials were keen for Chris to spend some time on their problems, so he felt comfortable about proceeding.

He decided on a project entitled: 'How should the Thornton Heath BSAC expand in order to secure its long-term survival?'

The project included a careful analysis of the market and the club, a survey of existing members and a detailed look at the financial implications of expansion. It gained a grade A.

# How to decide on a title

It is important to have a clear working title from early on in the project process. A clear title is one which keeps you focused and helps you explain quickly what you are trying to find out. A good example might be 'Should WH Smith in Barnsley open an in-store café?' Everyone inside and outside the business can understand from this title what you are doing and how **they** might be able to help.

So how do you decide on a title? There are three key issues to remember:

**1    A title must signal the type of project being tackled, e.g. 'A comparative study ...'.**

**This hardly seems worth saying, but in fact many assignments have titles which leave their purpose unclear. As an example, one title actually submitted for the AQA coursework was 'Anjelika's Music'. This sounds descriptive, and indeed it was.**

**In essence there are only three types of A level project:**

**i    a comparative study**

**ii   a feasibility study**

**iii  a project focused at an existing company's next steps, or at solving a problem it has; in this case the title is usually of the form 'Should ABC expand ...'.**

**Make sure that your working title sets out the type of project you have opted for.**

**2    The title must look forward towards the project's conclusions (e.g. 'Should Manchester United open a club shop in London?')**

**The key phrase here is look forward. Good projects only use the past to help understand the present and forecast the future. A project which is about a past problem or decision can do little more than describe what happened. It could be argued that there is a great deal to be learned from past mistakes. Every exam board would agree with that,**

but nevertheless the focus in business studies coursework is on the future not the past.

The title must reflect this focus on the future. It should point towards the conclusion or recommendation the reader can expect at the end. Take the title 'Should Manchester United open a club shop in London?' One knows from the outset that the author must end up with a yes or no, supported by evidence and argument. Such a title will help you to stay focused and help others to understand exactly what you are attempting to achieve.

3    The title must be sufficiently open to encourage an answer based upon judgement as well as numerical analysis. Take for example the title 'Can Mile End newsagency boost its profit by increasing its prices by 10%?' This title seems worthwhile, but it leads to only a yes/no answer. Where is the scope for judgement? Either it can or cannot. A better title would be 'Should Mile End newsagency increase its prices by 10%? The impact on profit would clearly be a key consideration, but there might be other factors to consider, such as the risk of attracting more competition.

As a general rule, the word 'should' is helpful in project titles.

## WHAT IS THE DIFFERENCE BETWEEN A WORKING TITLE AND THE FINAL TITLE?

A working title provides focus during your research process. It may have to be changed once or twice, for example if promised data never arrives. Such a change is no problem.

When your research is gathered and you are writing up the material, you may realise that the title is not quite right. It may not quite tie in with your objectives or with the type of conclusion you have drawn. Therefore you may need a new, final title.

The final title will be on the front cover of your research assignment and will influence the examiners' expectations of what will be inside. It is also likely that, on reaching the end of your text, examiners will return to the front cover to make sure that your project has achieved its aims. So make sure that the final title is a true reflection of how your assignment has ended up.

A B C D E F G H I J K L M N O P Q R S T U V W X Y Z

## Projects in Practice

Claire started work on a project entitled 'Developing a model to forecast Fulham FC home attendance figures, to help the club improve its profitability and chances of survival.' This working title helped her get interviews with the club's general manager, programme editor and safety officer. She found out the wastage level on programme printing, the costs of hiring police, wardens and turnstile operators and much else. Then Fulham FC was bought by Mohammed-al-Fayed. Suddenly Fulham's fight for financial survival seemed irrelevant. The new owner's top priority was crowd safety, security and convenience (to prevent unfavourable publicity). Worse came when the staff who had helped Claire were replaced by newcomers. Her access to data was halted. Her final title was 'Would a new model for forecasting home attendance figures help Fulham achieve its organisational objectives'. This was a considerable change from the working title, but led to a successfully completed project.

## HOW DO I KNOW WHAT MY WORKING TITLE SHOULD BE?

One of the first questions students are likely to be asked by their project contact is 'What is the project about?' The answer to this must be 'I have to do a problem solving or decision making assignment, so I need to come in and find out about your business. Then we can discuss what would make a good project'. Inevitably, your project title must wait until you have spent some time at the company (or talking with your contact). Only then can you (and your teacher) come up with a worthwhile title. Chapter 3 explains how to set about this process.

As it is unnerving to meet a business person without a clear idea of what you are after, it can be useful to start with a working title based on 'Conducting an analysis of the firm's strengths, weaknesses, opportunities and threats', often referred to as SWOT analysis. After completing this, you should be able to highlight an area of the business which you think would make a worthwhile, interesting assignment. Examples of working titles stemming from a SWOT analysis include:

- How should the DDB Co. reduce its debtors total?

- Why is ADG Co.'s labour turnover so high?

- Are FG's quality circles proving effective?

- Should Gino's Pizza expand the restaurant to the second floor?

- How should Chester Garage respond to the opening of a Tesco hypermarket and petrol outlet a mile away?

Each title emerged from discussions with the project contact and with others at the firm. Working titles can be changed or developed later. In the short term, they provide the student and the company with a clear idea of the scope and relevance of the assignment. Therefore they help convince staff that the student's task is worthwhile. Few managers are willing to devote much time to a project which seems to lead nowhere. Choosing an effective working title overcomes this and should be a major objective from the first visit to the contact company.

# Your first visit to the contact company

A good project teaches the reader or examiner a great deal about the business it is based on. Weak reports give the reader no more insight than a newspaper article. Your task is to get a terrific grasp of the business, its triumphs and its problems. The challenge is to learn how the company operates day by day, the quality of its management, what plans there are for the future and how well equipped the organisation is to achieve these ambitions.

All this will not be achieved on the first visit, but this is the time to start probing as to how the firm works. If your contact is reluctant to answer questions at this stage, you may need to look elsewhere.

For this first visit, when you may feel hesitant and the project focus is unclear, it is helpful to use the structure of a SWOT analysis. In other words, question your contact about the firm's strengths, weaknesses, opportunities and threats (SWOT). Within each of these four categories make sure to find out:

- **What are the company's main SWOTs**
- **Have they changed in recent years? If so, which ones and why?**
- **Is each SWOT unique to this business or shared by competitors?**
- **Which is the firm's single greatest SWOT? Why do you say that?**

Within this process, make sure to get full coverage across the functions of the business, i.e. apply it to marketing, finance, personnel and operations management. Your own contact may be a personnel manager so your project may end up focused on a personnel issue, but if you don't know the firm's financial position your project will lack depth and insight.

Having conducted the SWOT analysis, you should be in a position to ask your contact 'Do you think that any of these issues would make a good project?' A project may look at how a weakness can be overcome, an opportunity exploited, a strength turned into a key competitive advantage, or a threat planned for. Ideally, you want to come away from this meeting with a list of three or four possibilities which you can discuss with your tutor.

Before your appointment ends, try to agree the following principles behind your project work:

- **Numerical data will be made available to give a quantitative basis for your decisions or recommendations (the issue of confidentiality is dealt with on page 177).**

- **Good projects come from a range of sources of information; therefore it would be useful to meet/interview other managers.**

- **You will need to visit for several days quite soon, and then return in a few months time to tie up any loose ends (the idea here is to apologise in advance if other study commitments prevent you from maintaining regular contact).**

- **You accept without question the firm's right to see your report and have confidential items deleted; furthermore you would value feedback on the report from your contact (an assessment of this feedback can make an excellent conclusion to your assignment).**

## PRACTICAL ISSUES RELATING TO THE FIRST VISIT

Prepare carefully for this visit, not only because you want to impress your contact, but also for the information it will provide you with. How will you ensure you don't forget what has been said? You could write notes as the conversation proceeds, but perhaps this will slow things down; you may struggle to keep the questions coming. The ideal solution is to take a tape recorder. Ask at the outset for permission to use it. If your contact agrees, it will solve the problem of note taking and you will find that the recorder is soon forgotten.

There are other ways of preparing:

- **If the company is a plc, obtain its annual report and accounts (and read them) before going; your background knowledge will impress the contact.**

- **Prepare a list of questions based upon the SWOT analysis, but also designed to obtain:**

    **i**    **a brief overview of the company and its history**

    **ii**    **a management hierarchy/organisation chart, with your contact's position marked and explained**

    **iii**    **your contact's job description, plus an account of her/his employment history**

**iv** details of the number of sites/outlets the firm has, plus recent sales and profit trends (for at least five years).

Within a day of the visit, start typing up your notes and conclusions. The longer you wait, the hazier it will all seem. You will never remember what was said (and why) better than you do now.

## Projects in Practice

Clara was a shy girl for whom the first project visit was a very daunting experience. The contact was a friend of her parents who she did not know particularly well. After much delay she wrote suggesting a couple of days in the Easter holiday. She received a very encouraging letter back, agreeing a date.

To prepare for the day, she wisely wrote up a page of interview questions. These would enable her to keep things going after the SWOT analysis was complete. She intended to find out everything she could about her contact. What exactly were his responsibilities, his position, his expertise and his ambitions?

Armed with her notes, Clara found interviewing her contact surprisingly easy. She had taken a tape recorder, which proved no barrier to open conversation. The contact spent nearly two hours chatting, covering all that Clara would need as background. Helpfully, he suggested that Clara should spend the afternoon with a young management trainee who had spent a month in each of the firm's departments. This proved invaluable, as not only were the trainee's insights helpful, but also the trainee was to carry on being very supportive of Clara in the months that followed.

# Getting the most from your contact company

## 4.1 Contact or contacts?

You are embarked on a research assignment. Research is an attempt at finding the truth. What do consumers really want? What do managers really do? And so on. When journalists are researching a story they believe they have found the truth when they hear the same story from two independent sources. Project research within a firm is similar.

If you only hear about a firm's recent product launch from the sales manager, you may hear a tale of great marketing success. A separate conversation with the research and development manager might give a totally different impression. He may indicate that the product's unique selling point was poorly advertised, but the product's strengths pulled sales through despite the marketing department. Who is right? You will only be sure if you hear people from many different departments saying the same thing. More probably, you will remain unsure of the truth; all you will know is that the sales manager's view cannot be presented as fact.

The point of this is simple. If you want to write convincingly about a firm, you want more than one viewpoint. Even if your dad is the sales manager, and he would never lie to you (or exaggerate? What, never?) you will still benefit from more than one viewpoint. This will give you the different versions of events which provide you with the scope to analyse and evaluate. With one viewpoint, all you can do is repeat or describe. With two or more views, you have vastly more scope for showing your analytical strengths.

So throughout your time at the contact company, try hard to get as many appointments as possible. Of course, beware of stirring up problems by, for example, telling the research and development manager 'Ah, but the sales manager said ...'; you should never repeat a conversation in a gossipy way.

## 4.2 Been there? Seen that?

However good your contacts are at explaining things, there is no substitute for direct experience. If your project is on a sweet shop, can you spend a day working there? If the air-conditioning firm you are working on has a factory, can you go and visit? If it has a sales force, can you spend a day going out to meet clients? You may dread this kind of exposure, but:

**a    examiners love to hear about such experiences**

**b    you will gain more and richer perspectives about your contact firm**

**c    you will be able to fill up a page or two of project text.**

A top-class research assignment gives the reader a deep insight into the workings of a business. It gives the impression of a student who has the initiative, enthusiasm and personality to unlock doors, to see the business from various sides and thereby obtain a full picture. Really good projects require more than just sitting at a computer.

## Projects in Practice

David's working title was 'Should XXX plc's Warrington division pursue BS 5750?' His uncle worked for the company's head office, where David spent two days. He heard about the division's poor reputation for quality and the need to jolt the local management into taking quality seriously. Pressed by his teacher, David asked to go (and was sent, expenses paid) to the Warrington factory.

Taken round by an assembly supervisor, David was astounded to see old, dirty machinery and to hear his guide's contempt for the head office: 'We've had two detailed proposals for new investment turned down. They talk quality but do nothing.'

David's title changed to 'How can XXX plc improve quality at its Warrington plant?' and the content included an interesting account of the different perspectives from the local factory and head office management.

## 4.3  But what's my project about?

After a few days at a firm, many students are up to their ears in facts, figures and opinions about the company. Yet they still have no idea what their project title should be. As mentioned in Chapter 3, organising the data into a SWOT analysis can be very helpful. Let's assume, however, that still no title has emerged, or, perhaps worse, several titles have emerged but you cannot decide which to adopt.

You may find it helpful to analyse your findings in a grid such as Table 4.1. This should help identify which syllabus area to focus your project on. Then you can narrow it down to a specific title. You could tick the relevant boxes and add up the ticks. Another approach is to give each criterion a score out of ten. For example, for getting detailed figures from the company: a project on the company's profit would be very difficult and score 0, but labour turnover should be easy to obtain, and so score 8. Table 4.1 shows the latter method in comparing a project on profit versus one on labour turnover. It then applies the ticks method to motivation versus cash flow.

To produce the grid, put the possible project areas across the top and then judge each one on the eight criteria listed down the side. The one with the highest mark is the winner.

Note that this form of analysis would be worth including in your project report – probably within the background section.

**Table 4.1** Grid for analysing project ingredients, to help identify a project title

| | Profit | Labour turnover | Motivation | Cash flow |
|---|---|---|---|---|
| *Internal* | | | | |
| 1 Detailed figures | 0 | 8 | ✔ | ✔ |
| 2 Helpful contacts | 6 | 8 | | ✔ |
| 3 Scope for research survey | 4 | 10 | ✔ | |
| *External* | | | | |
| 4 Good background data | 10 | 6 | | ✔ |
| 5 Relevant theory which can be applied | 10 | 9 | ✔ | |
| 6 Scope for research survey | 8 | 2 | | |
| *Personal* | | | | |
| 7 Of interest to me | 5 | 8 | ✔ | |
| 8 Syllabus area I'm good at | 6 | 7 | ✔ | |
| Total | 49/80 | 58/80 | 5/8 | 3/8 |

## Projects in Practice

Mehul's uncle was a director of a small machine tools company. The uncle was hugely interested in the project and helped to identify three possible project areas:

i  export sales and marketing
ii  investment in new computer-aided manufacturing equipment
iii  increasing staff involvement and motivation.

Mehul's inclination was towards the third option, but he took the titles back to college to discuss them with his tutor. The tutor helped draft out the following grid.

|   | **Exporting** | **Investment** | **Staff involvement** |
|---|---|---|---|
| 1  Good background figures | 8 | 9 | 3 |
| 2  Detailed figures | 10 | 8 | 3 |
| 3  Helpful contacts | 8 | 10 | 6 |
| 4  Scope for research survey | 4 | 6 | 10 |
| 5  Relevant theory can be applied | 6 | 10 | 10 |
| 6  Of personal interest | 4 | 2 | 10 |
| 7  Suits my strengths | 4 | 8 | 8 |
| Total (out of 70) | 44 | 53 | 50 |

Having seen this, the tutor advised Mehul to go for the staff involvement project (viewing the investment option's higher score as too marginal). The student decided in favour of the investment project though, on the grounds that it had a better chance of generating a high grade. The project yielded a grade B, justifying Mehul's decision.

## 4.4  Before leaving

A classic mistake with projects is to gather large quantities of data during time spent at a firm, then disappear. The firm expects you to work on the material straight away. If there are queries, they are expected within a week or two. Meanwhile, you relax into post-fieldwork smugness! You may feel you've cracked the project and enjoy hearing about fellow students who are still struggling to find a contact, let alone complete the research. The problem is compounded for those whose fieldwork is in June or July. They usually vow to return to the material after the summer holiday.

There are two problems to consider. The first is your relationship with the company/your contact. You probably made your visit seem urgent in July but how can you phone up three months later and say 'Excuse me, but what did you mean by market mobility?' So, the first thing is to make sure the firm knows before you leave, that your timescale is quite long, and that you may not be in touch for a few months.

The second problem is strictly your own. Information which seems crystal clear at the time vanishes from the brain alarmingly quickly. You will forget what the personnel manager said if you do not type it up quickly. And even your typed-up version will mean less and less to you as the months pass.

Prepare your contact for any delay. Explain that you are going on holiday and may struggle when going through the material in the autumn. Warn that you may then need to pop in to clarify a few points and so avoid being prevented by embarrassment from making the phone call. Above all, do not follow the example outlined below (by one of my own students).

## Projects in Practice

James was a big-talking, bright student. His parents knew a self-made millionaire who had started a computer software business specialising in £50,000+ programs for the insurance industry. In early July, James spent a week at the firm. He met all the directors, spent a day with the sales force, was given access to every figure he asked for and in short, had the project 'on a plate'. The following Monday, James explained to the class all that he found out and all that he was going to do. That night, at parents' evening, his mother spoke with pride about how impressed their friend had been.

All through the autumn James was asked for project work; he always stalled, but said it was all in hand. Finally, in February, he owned up to having done nothing with the material, and being unable even to remember what he was supposed to be doing. Eventually, very embarrassed,

**Continued**

he phoned the family friend. He was civil, but not willing to spend ages going over material a second time.

James, with a potentially superb project, ended up with none at all.

A
B
C
D
E
F
G
H
I
J
K
L
M
N
O
P
Q
R
S
T
U
V
W
X
Y
Z

# ✓ Checklist 1

## Am I prepared?

These are the tasks you should tackle early on in the project process. They should be completed six months before your deadline for project completion. Use the checklist to see how you are getting on. Note that the project objectives may only become clear later on.

|  | Yes | Partly | No |
|---|---|---|---|
| **1** Discussed possible contacts with: | | | |
| Family | ☐ | ☐ | ☐ |
| Employers/at work | ☐ | ☐ | ☐ |
| Other contacts | ☐ | ☐ | ☐ |
| **2** Visited contact(s) to discuss: | | | |
| Areas of interest | ☐ | ☐ | ☐ |
| Access to company data | ☐ | ☐ | ☐ |
| Access to other staff (e.g. other employees, managers and/or branches) | ☐ | ☐ | ☐ |
| **3** Agreed a programme with contact: | | | |
| Appointments with several staff and managers | ☐ | ☐ | ☐ |
| Agreed a timetable (e.g. for preparing, approving and piloting a questionnaire) | ☐ | ☐ | ☐ |
| Know exactly what you're doing and when | ☐ | ☐ | ☐ |

|  | Agreed | Discussed | Not done |
|---|---|---|---|
| **4** Project objectives: | | | |
| Primary | ☐ | ☐ | ☐ |
| Secondary | ☐ | ☐ | ☐ |

# How to decide on your objectives

Getting crystal clear objectives is the single most important influence on a project's success. Objectives are the work's driving force and its cement, pushing it forward and binding it together. Ideally, an objective should be a measurable target with a specific timescale. For example:

'To eliminate XXX Ltd's £50,000 overdraft by the end of the year'

The above example sounds obvious, but the student concerned spent months working on the brief set by her project contact, which was to 'See how we could improve our cash flow'. The problem of this was its open-ended nature. There are masses of ways cash flow can be improved, and any improvement from £1 to £1 million would meet the contact's requirements. It was only when the above objective was agreed that she began to see how the assignment could be completed. (The final recommendations from this project are set out on page 101.)

## 5.1 Topics are not objectives

If at all possible, you should try to find a specific yardstick against which your recommendations can be judged. Then it is clear to you and the examiner whether your goals have been achieved. This can boost your mark directly, but even more important are the indirect benefits to you. Many students get bogged down in their project because they cannot see where it is leading. They gather lots of material which proves of little relevance. This wastes time and is dispiriting. So they push the work to one side until the final deadline (and the tutor) screams at them. A clear yardstick helps to prevent this. It ensures that you know when to stop. So whatever your project title, think of a plausible benchmark against which to judge it.

The table below provides a series of project topics, together with relevant yardsticks. Notice how much more specific (and therefore answerable) are the statements on the right.

| Project topic | Objective/yardstick |
|---|---|
| A supermarket's personnel officer is concerned about high levels of labour turnover. | Reduce the Fareham branch's labour turnover to the 8.5% average for the South East region. |
| A tennis club is concerned about falling revenue. | Boost revenue for next year to the £88,000 peak achieved two years ago. |
| A hospital is concerned about the queues in its accident and emergency outpatients department. | Ensure that, 95% of the time, patients queue for no longer than one hour. |
| A feasibility study into opening a Chinese fast food outlet (McChina). | Generate a long-term return on capital exceeding 30% – the minimum my uncle demands to invest the start-up capital. |
| A small manufacturing firm is thinking of applying for BS 5750 quality certification. | Can FDG Ltd achieve BS 5750 with one manager taking no more than 20 weeks and spending no more than £4000? |

Each objective set out on the right is precise enough to give clear direction to an entire project. It is therefore the primary objective. When you have determined your primary objective, what comes next?

The primary objective must be broken down into secondary objectives, each of which is a smaller, more manageable target. When each of these is answered, the primary objective as a whole will have been met. For example, look below at how the BS 5750 Project objectives could be broken down.

## Projects in Practice

### 1 Primary objective

Can FDG Ltd achieve BS 5750 with one manager taking no more than 20 weeks and spending no more than £4000?

Continued

## 2 Secondary objectives

2.1 Identify the key elements of FDG Ltd's work which require quality monitoring

2.2 Discover the experiences of other small manufacturers who have pursued BS 5750:
  - those who achieved the award
  - and those who withdrew or failed

2.3 Identify the procedures required for BS 5750 approval

2.4 Decide the amount and type of work required to get the approval and estimate the man hours it will take

2.5 Determine whether the manager allotted to the task can achieve it in the time available

2.6 Estimate the costs to be incurred in the approval process

Reading through the secondary objectives gives a clear idea of the activities the student will undertake.

## 5.2 Establishing a primary objective

The primary objective for a project should be rooted in the project title. It is quite possible that the title and primary objective will be identical. Often, though, the title is an aim (a generalised statement of intent) whereas the primary objective is very specific.

The table below shows a range of possibilities. Some of the titles are very vague, but all the objectives give a specific idea of what the assignment is trying to achieve. Better candidates will base much of their conclusions on evaluating how well their findings and recommendations meet their objectives.

| Project title | Primary objectives |
|---|---|
| An investigation of CPS Ltd. | Should CPS Ltd expand and, if so, how? |
| The quest for Solarium. | Sales of Solarium fragrance have been falling for the last four years. Although ambitious, my objective is to restore sales to their former level. |
| Is it feasible to start up a colour cosmetics shop in the Whitgift Centre? | To make fully justified recommendations on the financial feasibility of starting up a colour cosmetics shop in the Whitgift Centre. |
| Investigating the English wine industry. | Examining the feasibility of setting up a vineyard in England which grows its own grapes and has its own winery. |
| How can profit be maximised at Mona Stores to generate the highest possible price for selling the business? | How can profit be maximised at Mona Stores to generate the highest possible price for selling the business? |
| Is there a market gap for a travel firm specialising in fashion holidays? | To determine the financial viability of starting up a new tour operator offering fashion holidays. |

Objectives lay down the direction your researches will take. They therefore require a great deal of time, thought and discussion. A mistake means heading off in the wrong direction and almost certainly wastes time.

Yet setting an objective is by no means easy. This is largely because, at the outset, you know too little to decide what would be the right objective. It may only be after a few days in the firm, finding out who is helpful and who is not, that you can identify the part of the business which is potentially of most interest. Even if you then embark on an assignment, the promised data may not be forthcoming.

It is quite normal for four weeks to elapse before the project objective becomes clear. When you feel you are close to deciding your primary objective, bear in mind the following pointers.

## The dos and don'ts of primary objectives

| Project dos | Project don'ts |
|---|---|
| ☑ Make sure the objective looks to the future. | ☒ Do not set an objective which looks back at a past decision or problem. |
| ☑ Keep it short and highly specific – the detail will emerge in the secondary objectives. | ☒ Avoid lengthy, 'chuck everything in' objectives. |
| ☑ The objective must be realistic – keep it small and keep it local. | ☒ Do not assume that top grades come from amazingly ambitious projects. |
| ☑ Do check the objective with your project contact – to ensure that it will not cause problems of confidentiality or office politics; also discuss it with your tutor. | ☒ Avoid the disappointment of hearing (late on) that the firm is unwilling to help with the objective you have set; discuss objectives before setting them. |
| ☑ Try to ensure your objective has a specific yardstick with a measurable timescale. | ☒ Don't set open-ended objectives; they lead to open-ended (or never ending!) research. |

## 5.3 Establishing secondary objectives

In many ways, this is an easier task. Once the primary objective is clear, the secondary objectives should fall into place.

Secondary objectives are the goals required to meet the primary objective. In effect, they are arrived at by breaking the primary objective down into its component parts. For example, if the primary objective is to carry out an investment appraisal, the component parts might be:

* **identifying the initial costs of the investment**

* **forecasting the level of cash inflows and outflows**

* **establishing a timescale for the initial costs, the net cash flows and the ending of the investment's lifetime**

* **analysing the overall cash flows using investment appraisal techniques**

* **evaluating the results against the firm's capital appraisal criteria.**

What the above example illustrates is that secondary objectives often flow naturally and logically from the overall (primary) goal. The skill is to break down the overall objective into its component parts. This is relatively easy when you have already studied the theory concerned, for example investment appraisal in the above case. But what if you are tackling a project on a topic you have not yet studied (or remember so poorly as to make no difference)? The following procedure may be helpful:

1  **Find a book on the subject. There are an enormous number of 'how to' books in business studies. A project might have the objective 'Assess the effectiveness of GJT's performance appraisal in order to recommend improvements'. A quick look through a book on appraisal (there are lots of them) will help you see how to break your overall goal down into sub-objectives. To help you with this, a general list of books for tackling specific project objectives is given in the A–Z of useful resources on page 203. Note that coursework marking favours those who use several sources of information and those who incorporate theory into their practical project. You have a chance to achieve both at once.**

2  **Discuss the sub-objectives with your tutor and your project contact. This is important, but beware of taking a back seat. If the detailed objectives are dictated to you (fathers are the worst for this) it is unlikely you will shine in the research that follows. You are the one who has to do the hard, perhaps boring, work of gathering information. If you are not clear *why* you are doing it, you will never find sufficient motivation. So discuss; don't just accept the ideas of others.**

3  **Analyse. Just think it through. In order to assess the firm's employee appraisal system, you might need to:**

   i    **know what the appraisal is for (the objectives of the firm's scheme)**

   ii   **determine the way it is carried out**

   iii  **determine the way it is carried out elsewhere (especially if your project is a comparative study)**

   iv   **discover what managers think of the current scheme**

   v    **discover what staff think of the current scheme**

   vi   **identify what changes are desirable and practical**

   vii  **assess the costs of making the changes you recommend.**

To do this effectively, just keep asking yourself 'then what? then what? then what?' Keep remembering that objectives are about 'what' and don't get confused with 'how?', which concerns the method you will use to achieve your objectives.

| What? (objective) | How? (method) |
|---|---|
| To determine the way appraisal is carried out ... | observe an appraisal interview; discuss the method with the personnel officer. |
| To determine the way appraisal is carried out elsewhere ... | contact the Institute of Personnel Development (IPD) to obtain a research report on the general use of appraisal in businesses today. |
| To discover what managers think of the current scheme ... | write a questionnaire and supply it to each of the 43 managers; press for speedy return of this self-completion questionnaire. |
| To assess the costs ... | calculate the personnel management time and the paperwork cost involved in changing the system; cost it in relation to the personnel department's budget. |

## Projects in Practice

Raj's project focused on rebuilding the family business's once-successful fragrance Solarium.

### Primary objective

Sales of Solarium have been falling for the last four years. Although ambitious, my objective is to restore sales to their former level.

### Secondary objectives

1 Examine the reasons for the decline in sales of Solarium.

**Continued**

2 Gather background research to identify the correct market positioning for Solarium.

3 Calculate the number of consumers within the relevant market segment.

4 Develop alternative marketing strategies to achieve the primary objective.

5 Choose the best marketing approach, then assess its ability to rebuild sales.

6 Identify how the finance is to be raised to fund the relaunch of Solarium.

7 Evaluate the findings of the sales forecast, investment appraisals and market research.

# How to establish an effective method

A method is a plan for meeting your objectives. Having decided on your project objectives, you must find a way of achieving them that is businesslike, practical and enables you to meet the academic demands of A level coursework.

## 6.1 Matching the method to the objectives

Having clarified your primary and secondary objectives, write down the method by which you will achieve each one. As you do so, bear in mind that high marks require the use of a variety of sources, both primary and secondary. In other words, if your method for achieving objective number 1 is 'discussion with management', try to think of a different way to meet the second objective. This should not be impossible, because there is no shortage of possible methods as illustrated below.

| **Requirement** | **Methods available** |
|---|---|
| To obtain background information | *primary:* interviews with management, interviews with customers, factory visit, work shadowing, observation<br>*secondary:* annual reports, company accounts, newspaper articles, government data, trade press articles |
| To obtain marketing data | *primary:* interview retail buyers, survey of existing or potential customers, accompany a sales rep on visits to customers<br>*secondary:* analyse sales figures, use market intelligence reports |

| | |
|---|---|
| To gain information within the firm | *primary:* face to face interviews with key staff, attend meetings (especially consultation meetings), self-completion staff questionnaires *secondary:* read application forms, analyse staff newsletter/newspaper, read reports on topics related to yours |
| To obtain cost information | *primary:* visit commercial estate agents, look at advertisements in local/national press (e.g. for wage rates), phone suppliers, ask comparable firms (no one minds giving information such as electricity bills or water rates) *secondary:* analyse company accounts (e.g. divide Pizza Express wage costs by their number of branches to find wage bill per pizza outlet). |

## 6.2 Ensuring the use of varied methods

If your personal objective is to study management at a good university, which method would you adopt? You would get advice from the careers department and from your tutor. You would look up relevant universities in the various books and newspaper articles. You might visit one or two universities, to get the feel of them. While there, you would be wise to ask not only the lecturers, but also current students, to find out their views. You might look up the official ratings of the universities' research and teaching standards (are they *really* excellent?) By the time you fill out your UCAS form you should know exactly what you want. Your research method should have put you in a good position to make a correct decision.

Business coursework is the same. The key to success in the above example is the variety of sources of information. You should not commit three years of your life on the basis of one person's view or one (perhaps out of date) book. A mixture of reading (secondary) and visiting (primary) experience makes it far more likely that you will arrive at a good decision.

So do not rely solely on one person's view, or on one report's data. A varied method leads to more interesting findings, often more complex and contradictory in nature.

**Projects in Practice**

Mark's project was to recommend how a fast-growing firm should reorganise its factory to improve efficiency and increase capacity. His uncle the works manager was keen to help. When first shown round, Mark's uncle explained about various inefficiencies. Instead of just accepting these, Mark asked if he could follow an order through the factory. When he did this, he found the order took six days to complete, even though the work time spent on production and packing only amounted to five hours. The rest of the time was wasted in stockpiles, as the order waited to be processed through each part of the job. When chatting to one or two of the machine operators Mark found out that the production schedules were often disorganised. Gradually he was building up a very different, richer view of the workings of the factory. The project's eventual grade A was fully deserved.

## 6.3 Identifying a method which is academically valid

To achieve a high grade at coursework, an academic approach is vital. In other words your method must convince the reader that you have approached your project through techniques worthy of A level standard. If your source material is complex, and requires difficult analysis, this may be easy to demonstrate. In most cases though, the material is relatively straightforward, so it is necessary to plan a method which will impress.

To illustrate this point, here are two examples:

**1   Complex topic; straightforward method**
Richard tackled a stock control project, in which he had to devise a method of stock ordering which would reduce the capital tied up in stock while reducing out-of-stock levels. He achieved this by constructing a model based on the cost of the stock, the frequency of usage and the delivery time. The net result was a plan which would reduce the stock value by £32,000 (15%) but (according to the student) result in fewer instances of running out of stock. This complex project was greatly appreciated by the company and gained an A for the student.

2 **Straightforward topic; complex method**

Sejal's project was a business start-up, in which sales and costs had to be forecast from scratch. Here the need was for a method with high academic demands. This was achieved by a complex method for ensuring as accurate a sales forecast as possible. She devised three methods for forecasting sales, then weighed up how best to use her results. She rejected an average of the three in favour of the lowest (most prudent) result. Her three methods were:

i     a quantitative survey of the opinions of potential customers

ii    the sales average for the type of business (market value divided by the number of outlets)

iii   an estimate based on traffic flow past this outlet compared with that of a similar outlet for which annual sales were known.

The following, then, are the key characteristics of an academic method:

1   It should be capable of being reproduced: in other words the examiner should have enough detailed information to be able to copy the research method used. A good example is that students often say 'My survey was carried out using a quota sample', yet give no indication of how the quotas were decided on and what they were. Were they 40% men, 60% women or the reverse? And most importantly why? So give exact details of your method.

2   It should be objective: meaning that the method and your use of the method should be unbiased.

3   It should gain more than one viewpoint: so that the truth is more likely to emerge.

4   It should apply correct theory to planning, conducting, analysing and evaluating quantitative research: special consideration should be given to the type and size of sample, and the response rate.

5   The research should be genuine: phoney research is easy to spot and undermines the credibility of your whole assignment.

# 6.4 Rethinking the method on a project which has gone adrift

Obvious though this heading sounds, the difficulties involved here should not be underestimated. Most business contacts are keen to tell a visitor everything about their job, their successes and their problems. This can be helpful if it provides an understanding of the business, but is nothing directly to do with a business project. The project, of course, is about a future decision or solution to a currently unresolved problem.

When, eventually, the assignment becomes focused upon suitable objectives, it is often so late that 3000 words or so have already been written. These are largely a description of the business (from the contact's point of view). Even at this late stage it is sensible to be ruthless about your method. Cut back on the descriptive background and make sure that you find a method for achieving your objectives. If a sales forecast is essential as the basis of a cash flow forecast, find a way to make one, even if it means making an estimate. Material which is relevant but estimated is preferable to accurate but irrelevant description.

## Combining objectives and method

A useful approach is to combine objectives and method in the same section. As the following example shows, such a procedure makes it particularly easy to see the logic behind the project. It is also a useful way of pruning down your text if the word count is too high.

### Projects in Practice

### Title: Should XXX Motors purchase a long-term lease on its premises?

### Project objectives

#### *Main objective*

1 To examine the implications for XXX Motors if they were to purchase a long leasehold

#### *Secondary objectives*

2 To assess the firm's present financial position

*2.1 Method*

Using the company's accounts from 2000, 2001 and 2002 I intend to use ratio analysis to find out if XXX Motors has enough capital to purchase the lease, or if it

**Continued**

is in a position to borrow money from a lender. I will also be looking at the firm's liquidity position. To do this, I will be looking at the gross profit ratio, capital gearing ratio and acid test.

**3** To forecast the firm's likely financial position if the lease is not purchased

*3.1 Method*

Using the accounts from previous years I intend to forecast the firm's likely balance sheet and profit and loss account if the lease is not bought. I intend to conduct some primary research by interviewing the owners to find out if sales and costs are likely to increase or decrease over the following year. All figures will be estimates, although inflation will be taken into account.

**4** To forecast the likely increase in revenue if the expansion goes ahead

*4.1 Method*

Again using the accounts for the period 2000–2002 and primary research from 3, I will construct an estimated balance sheet and profit and loss account. Sales forecasts from my primary data will be used to help predict future sales revenues and costs.

**5** To construct a 2003 cash flow forecast if the lease is purchased

*5.1 Method*

If the lease is purchased, the firm's 2003 cash flow forecast will not be the same as if the lease is not purchased. Therefore, using the same figures calculated in 4, I will construct a cash flow forecast assuming that the lease is not purchased.

**6** To apply relevant investment appraisal techniques

*6.1 Method*

Using payback, net present value (NPV) and average rate of return (ARR) and with the aid of the forecast

**Continued**

cash flows calculated in 5, I intend to show the feasibility of buying the long-term lease

**7** To study all other qualitative factors that should be taken into account before a decision is made

### 7.1 Method

Using both primary and secondary research, other qualitative factors will be considered. Secondary data from newspapers and magazines will help predict the likely future in the market. Primary information gathered from the interview with the owners in 3 will give me their views on the strengths and weaknesses of the expansion.

**8** To make recommendations as to the course of action for XXX Motors concerning whether or not to buy the lease

### 8.1 Method

Using conclusions from 2 to 7, I intend to answer my initial objective.

**9** To evaluate my project, describe any problems encountered and explain how they were overcome

A B C D E F G H I J K L M N O P Q R S T U V W X Y Z

# Writing an effective background

## 7.1 What should the background section consist of?

Once the focus of your project is clear, you are in a position to write about the background to your assignment. Your goal here is to help the reader understand *why* you are undertaking this particular task. For example, if you are doing a project on boosting profitability at a jewellery shop, it would be helpful to know previous years' profitability figures, plus details of any past changes in policy or competition.

Often, the background section of a project is full of general information such as the company history and its organisational hierarchy. These facts may be important, but often they are included whether or not they are relevant. As a result, many backgrounds are long and boring. The reader wades through hundreds of words without knowing where they are leading. (Indeed, they may lead nowhere.)

Success comes from ensuring that every aspect of the background section helps lead the reader towards the project objectives. For instance, if the background gave details of the sad decline of a family business from profit to below breakeven, it would be appropriate to the objective 'To rebuild the trading position of Hollis & Co. to restore profits to their 2001 level'.

What, then, might a background contain? It depends, of course, on the project title. Here are some examples:

| Title | Background |
| --- | --- |
| A feasibility study into starting a kebab shop in Colchester. | 1 Explain why you're doing a feasibility study.<br>2 Explain why:<br>  i food<br>  ii a kebab shop<br>3 Explain the competition locally, including a map showing which rivals are where. |

| Should Friendly Stores invest in laser scanning equipment? | 1 Give a brief history of the shop's recent past including graphs of sales and profits over the last five years. |
| | 2 Explain Friendly Stores' main pattern of trade, whether steady or erratically busy. |
| | 3 Analyse the strengths and weaknesses of the shop, focusing on stock control and speed/efficiency at the checkout. |
| | 4 Look at the competition Friendly Stores faces locally. |
| Should XXX plc act to reduce its high staff turnover? | 1 Explain XXX plc's main lines of business. |
| | 2 Describe the main jobs carried out within the business. |
| | 3 Investigate competition facing the business, to assess the likely impact of high labour turnover. |

## 7.2 How should the background be written?

If possible, try to grab the reader's attention from the start. This can be done by dramatising (visually, perhaps) the difficulties of a company with financial problems, or by focusing upon a particularly interesting snippet of information from the company's recent history. The point is a simple one. Projects of between 3000 and 5000 words are hard – often dull – reading. So it is sensible to try to make the reader/examiner sit up and take notice of your assignment.

A further tip is to keep the text brief. Later on will come your opportunity to show your analytic and evaluative skills. The background is largely descriptive, so keep it short. The important marks are available for the work that comes later.

Make sure, though, that your background leads on to your objectives. This is necessary to give the project the coherence it needs to achieve high marks overall. See how the following example sweeps you towards the objectives with background material which is well researched and explained but, above all, relevant.

## Projects in Practice

## Title: Is it feasible to open up an Asian boutique in Thornton Heath?

*By: Kamal Kataria*

### 1 Hypothesis

Although there is a large Asian community in Thornton Heath (South London), most women go to Southall or Wembley to buy up to date ethnic clothing. A round trip to either place takes three hours, so I believe there may be an opportunity for a boutique in Thornton Heath.

### 2 Background research

- location
- secondary background research
- present competition

### 2.1 Location

My reasons for choosing Thornton Heath as a place to set up an Asian boutique are clear. The area has a high and growing Asian population (see Fig 7.1 below) and London Road, Thornton Heath Pond is a major Asian shopping area. I also believe that the four Asian boutiques in Thornton Heath do not cater to the needs of younger Asian women.

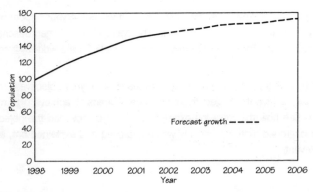

**Figure 7.1**

**Continued**

As you can see, the Asian population in Thornton Heath is growing all the time. Although future growth is forecast to slow, population growth at least is higher than for the UK population as a whole.

## 2.2 Secondary background research

From carrying out research on the womenswear market at the City Business Library, I found the market has been expanding, even though some feel it is saturated. Since 1998 the market value of clothes in general has increased 24.2%, but womenswear has increased 26.6% (look at Fig 7.2).

Retail sales of women's wear compared with all clothing (constant 1998 prices)

| Year | All clothing £m | Women's wear £m |
|------|------------------|-----------------|
| 1998 | 18,384 | 10,355 |
| 1999 | 19,544 | 11,100 |
| 2000 | 20,506 | 11,726 |
| 2001 | 21,404 | 12,723 |
| 2002 | 22,835 | 13,112 |
| % change (1998–2002) | 24.2% | 26.6% |

**Figure 7.2** (Source: City Business Library, Mintel Reports 2002)

I was able to get estimated figures of sales of women's clothing from the Namdhari Sikh Heritage Society. They told me that the market for Asian women's clothing was £2,256,840 in 2002 – an increase of 93% since 1998! These figures are for Southall and Wembley only, and contain information only from the leading boutiques in those areas. Fig 7.3 shows the difference between the growth of the Asian womenswear market and all womenswear.

**Continued**

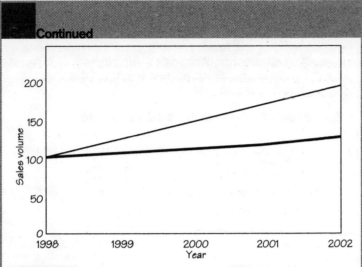

**Figure 7.3**

Discussion with boutique owners suggested three possible reasons for this dramatic growth in Asian womenswear:

- increasing fashion consciousness leading to more frequent purchasing of new styles
- increasing availability of clothes which would once have been bought only when visiting India or Pakistan
- increasing numbers of Asian women from throughout London coming to Southall and Wembley.

### *2.3 Present competition*

At the moment there are four Asian boutiques in Thornton Heath, but in my own opinion there is a gap in the market. Three of the outlets are more fabric shops than boutiques. The only actual boutique that sells newly designed Asian garments is Temptations, but this is quite small and has a restricted range. The only other local competition comes from Tooting, which is another Asian shopping area. However when I visited Tooting I found once again only Asian fabric shops. Discussion with my sisters confirmed that Temptations was the only nearby shop within my market sector. My business proposition was starting to seem promising.

# ✓ Checklist 2
## Am I clear?

These are the tasks you should tackle in the first half of the project process. They should be started four months before the deadline for project completion. Use the checklist to review your progress.

|  | Yes | Partly | No |
|---|---|---|---|
| **1**  Is my primary objective clear and agreed? | | | |
| With my project contact | ☐ | ☐ | ☐ |
| With my teacher/tutor | ☐ | ☐ | ☐ |
| **2**  Is the primary research method clear and agreed? | ☐ | ☐ | ☐ |
| Research method discussed and agreed | | | |
| Questionnaire written | ☐ | ☐ | ☐ |
| Questionnaire approved by contact | ☐ | ☐ | ☐ |
| Questionnaire piloted | ☐ | ☐ | ☐ |
| **3**  Has the project contact been willing to provide numerical data on: | | | |
| (You don't need all of these, just some willingness to provide internal data.) | | | |
| Sales figures/turnover over the past 5 years | ☐ | ☐ | ☐ |
| Company P&L Account and Balance Sheet | ☐ | ☐ | ☐ |
| Data such as labour turnover or R&D spending | ☐ | ☐ | ☐ |
| Other internal company data | ☐ | ☐ | ☐ |
| **4**  Have you returned to the company to discuss points of confusion or where more development is needed? | | | |
| With your company contact | ☐ | ☐ | ☐ |
| With other advisors/contacts | ☐ | ☐ | ☐ |

A B C D E F G H I J K L M N O P Q R S T U V W X Y Z

# Market research: effective secondary research

The reader/examiner of your project needs to understand the organisation's market background. If the assignment is about labour turnover problems at a hospital, the market research requirement will be very low: little more, perhaps, than a map showing any rival hospitals or doctors' surgeries. More often though, market research will be at the heart of the project. Secondary research will be needed to set the business decision within its context. A combination of primary and secondary research will often be used to quantify the effects of the decisions being evaluated.

Importantly, a great many of the skills being assessed by the examiners can be shown through market research. In other words, success here can have a great bearing on the final mark.

Secondary research means gathering data which has already been compiled, that is obtaining it second hand. Inevitably then, the research will not have been tailored to meet your own specific requirements. Fortunately, there are so many sources of secondary research that relevant material can often be found. But what exactly is there and how do you find it? This section explains generally about the data available. Chapter 9 goes on to explain specifically about primary research.

Secondary research falls into five main categories: national data, local data, market intelligence data, company/financial data and media information (articles, photos etc.) The following section outlines not only the information available, but also how it could be used in an assignment.

## 8.1 National data

### GOVERNMENT DATA

Government data covers a huge range, from economic data such as inflation trends, monthly car sales and consumer expenditure patterns through to population figures and crime statistics. Most libraries carry the key volumes of published data: *Annual Abstract of Statistics*, *Social Trends*, *Economic*

*Trends, Consumer Trends, Monthly Digest of Statistics* and *Labour Market Trends*. All are published by the Office of National Statistics. (Each costs about £50, so rely on your school, college or local library.)

| Project need | Source of information |
|---|---|
| Average annual percentage change in the number of 16–19-year-olds in next five years (for years 2–5 of a sales forecast for a new nightclub) | *Annual Abstract of Statistics* *Social Trends* |
| Trends in burglaries over past five years (background to the success of a home security company) | *Annual Abstract of Statistics* |
| Inflation over the past five years (to deflate a firm's sales turnover figures as described on page 95) | *Economic Trends* … and (for latest updates) *Monthly Digest of Statistics* or *Labour Market Trends* |
| Wage rates for chefs, waiters/waitresses and bar staff (to estimate wage bill for a new Beefeater) | *Labour Market Trends* |
| Trends in the percentage of households with satellite or cable TV (for project on setting up a black cable TV station) | *Social Trends* |
| Interest rates over past ten years (to explain why a firm needs to reduce its gearing level) | *Annual Abstract of Statistics* *Economic Trends* |

## OTHER NATIONAL DATA

The *Quarterly Industrial Trends Survey*, published by the Confederation of British Industry (CBI), is a goldmine of information. Its strength is that it covers relatively small industrial sectors such as machine tools or building materials. These are the areas which are not covered by the general market intelligence companies, so the CBI is filling a useful gap.

As an example, consider a student tackling a project on a plastics manufacturing company. She is looking at whether the firm should invest in new equipment for producing a new range of high-tech machinery. The company has kindly provided the necessary internal data, but she needs some secondary research to give the wider business context.

The CBI survey provides her with the following data:

**Table 8.1** CBI Industrial trends survey October 2002 (percentages)

|  | More | Same | Less |
|---|---|---|---|
| Are you more, or less, optimistic than you were four months ago about the general business situation in your industry? | | | |
|     Plastics manufacturers | 1 | 71 | 28 |
|     All companies in sample (912) | 15 | 51 | 34 |
| Do you expect to authorise more or less expenditure in the next 12 months than over the past 12 months on product and process innovation? | | | |
|     Plastics manufacturers | 11 | 70 | 16 |
|     All companies in the sample (912) | 24 | 54 | 19 |

This information enables the researcher to point out how low confidence is in the plastics manufacturing sector. This might lead her to place a relatively high capital investment criterion on the investment, in other words insist that the project should proceed only if the average rate of return is comfortably above the rate of interest.

## 8.2 Local data

The provision of local data will inevitably vary regionally. The only sources of local information that definitely exist everywhere are:

- **Yellow Pages/Thompson Local, listings of local firms, categorised by type of business (e.g. pizza take-away).**

- **the electoral register, which is especially useful for identifying 17–18-year-olds, perhaps for a postal survey**

- **local council information on planning permissions and enquiries, and on the population levels in local districts**

- **local estate agents' information on the availability of commercial properties and their prices/leasehold charges.**

In addition, you may find that your local library has a wealth of information, such as maps showing which firm is sited where in the high street, a breakdown of the local population by age, sex and occupation plus the contact details of local business groups such as the Chamber of Commerce. The library may also have back numbers of the local newspaper which may be helpful as a way of tracing when a key event happened, such as the opening of a by-pass or the closure of a large employer.

A further source of valuable local information is the government census. Many libraries hold this information, broken down into areas as small as electoral wards. These might contain a population of around 5000 people. Known as Small Area Statistics (SAS), this provides invaluable information on the age, ethnic and employment structure of your local district. This enables you to find out:

- **how many 15–24-year-olds live close to a café/bar you're thinking of opening**
- **how many Afro-Caribbean adults live in the area of your contact's music store**
- **how many pensioners live near the Community Centre you're researching into.**

| Project need | Source of information |
|---|---|
| Competitor analysis of all takeaway outlets in Harrogate (to plot on a map, to identify if any area of the town lacks takeaways) | *Thompson Local* *Yellow Pages* |
| Up to date information on the level of trade locally (is business booming?) for project background | local Chamber of Commerce local newspaper offices |
| Information on local wage rates | Job Centre job advertisements in local paper |
| Cost of leasing a shop in a prime high-street location compared with a back street | local estate agent with a commercial property section (see advertisements in local paper) |

## 8.3 Market intelligence data

Various commercial businesses produce detailed analyses of the major consumer and retail markets. These contain data on market size, market share, market trends, forecasts of future trends, distribution patterns, advertising spending and much, much more. In brief, just one of these reports can give you all the market background you are likely to need.

For example, in a recent project on opening a nightclub, the student was able to find out from a single Mintel report:

- **annual spending in the sector (over £2 billion!)**
- **the impact of the 1990–1992 recession (and thereby calculate the income elasticity of nightclubs)**
- **trends in the numbers of small and large clubs (small ones declining, large ones increasing)**
- **analysis of competition in the sector (showing exceptionally little dominance by any single company, therefore implying that a newcomer would have a chance)**
- **the growth forecast for nightclub admissions over the next four years.**

There are drawbacks, however. First, the reports are hugely expensive to buy: £300–800 for just one report on one market. This not only puts them out of your price bracket but also out of the reach of most libraries. Secondly, they may not provide really up to date information. Leading providers such as Mintel and Market Research of Great Britain assess four or five markets each month. They may only tackle the market you are interested in every three years. In which case, if you are unlucky, the data might be rather out of date. This matters relatively little in slow moving markets such as chocolate confectionery but in consumer electronics two years old is two years too late. Despite these reservations, it is worth repeating that just one of these reports can give you all the market background you are likely to need.

The main providers of market intelligence information are:

- **Mintel**
- **Key Notes**
- **Retail Business (now renamed Consumer Goods UK)**
- **Market Research Great Britain (MRGB).**

There is no reason to suppose you need more than one of these. Much of the data they contain is overlapping. The single most useful of the four is *Key Notes*, because it is updated on every major market every year.

A bigger issue is how can you find these reports. Unfortunately the answer is 'with difficulty'. You could expect only to find them in a major public library (such as Manchester Central), a business library (such as London's City Business Library) or within a university business school. Your school/college may be able to forge some links with the latter, but for you as an individual the first two are better bets.

To help you to identify where you can get hold of these reports there is a table on pages 196 and 197 showing which library holds what. The list was compiled for this book by sending a questionnaire to 50 major libraries from all over the UK. (Many thanks to the 47 who replied.) It was updated in early 2001.

It is worth looking at the list now to see whether a library near you holds this information.

Examples of the information requirements which can be met by market intelligence information are set out in the table below.

| Project need | Source of information |
| --- | --- |
| Recent trend in the annual value of alcoholic drink sales (to see whether the decline in family off-licence sales is typical of the whole market) | *Mintel* *Consumer Goods UK* *Key Notes* |
| Consumer/demographic profile of buyers of premium ice cream (to set a quota sample) | *Mintel* *Key Notes* |
| Advertising spending and the number of outlets per pizza company, to estimate the advertising spend per outlet (planning to open up a new pizza outlet) | *Key Notes* *Mintel* *Consumer Goods UK* |
| Calculating market shares in the fish finger market (for a project on an extension strategy for one of the major brands) | *Mintel* *Key Notes* |

In addition to these well-known sources of business information, it is important to remember that a great deal more data exists within every company and industry. Often the information is held by trade associations such as the British Soft Drinks Association or the Society of Motor Manufacturers & Traders.

A useful reference book to look for is *Sources of Unofficial UK Statistics* by D. Mort, published in 1997 by Gower Press. It gives details of over 870 sources of non-governmental information; some expensive, others free.

## 8.4 Company/financial data

There are five possible sources of company and financial data: the annual report and accounts, the data filed at Companies' House, Extel (now renamed Sequencer), published volumes of inter-firm ratio comparisons, and newspaper cuttings. The first three of these provide much the same information (a company's profit and loss account and balance sheet) so they can be grouped together. Newspaper articles and cuttings are dealt with on page 58.

## COMPANY ACCOUNTS

For public limited companies (those with plc after their names) the annual report and accounts is an essential document. In addition to the accounts, a great deal of information may be volunteered, such as how many outlets or factories there are, how sales break down by distribution outlet and many other possibilities. There are three main options for obtaining the annual report:

1   **Contact the firm's Head Office; plcs are usually keen to support business education.**

2   **Use the *Financial Times Annual Report Service*. Look at the share price listings near the back of the newspaper and make a note of any companies you are interested in which have a clubs symbol (♣) by the company name. Phone or fax the numbers given on the page and the Financial Times will post you any reports for firms with the clubs symbol free of charge.**

3   **Look in any large library or business library for a stock of company reports.**

With private limited companies (those with Ltd after their names), your best bet is to ask for the accounts and hope they are given. If not, there are various options:

1   **Use a directory of company finances; each covers over 10,000 companies, all listed alphabetically by company name. Bigger libraries are likely to have one or more of the following:**

i    Jordan's: *Britains Top Privately Owned Companies* ranks the top 10,000 companies in order of their net asset value. A great deal more data is provided. For example, if you were doing a feasibility study into opening a bookshop, it would be helpful to look up Books Etc. (a small chain) to discover its turnover, profit, gearing, liquidity, stock levels, wage bill and average pay per employee. (Jordan's Limited are at 21 St. Thomas Street, Bristol BS1 6JS, tel. 0117 923 0600.)

ii   *Kompass Financial Data* provides a similar service to Jordan's. It covers 30,000 firms, but gives less financial detail. (Published by Kompass, Reed Information Services, Windsor Court, East Grinstead RH19 1XD tel. 01342 326972.)

iii  *Waterlow's Unquoted Companies* covers 20,000 firms with turnovers in excess of £7 million. It provides very full information on company accounts. (Published by Jordan's (as above)

iv   *FAME (Financial Analysis Made Easy)* is a CD-ROM produced by Jordan's containing data on 270,000 major public and private companies with an annual turnover greater than £500,000. The database can provide ratio analysis within sectors chosen by you, for example for companies supplying computer software. It also provides data on individual firms. For example, it showed in December 2002 that Fulham Football Club (1987) Ltd had grown as follows:

| Year | Turnover £000 | Staff | Year | Turnover £000 | Staff |
|------|------|------|------|------|------|
| 1996 | 1,428 | 53 | 2000 | 7,560 | 310 |
| 1997 | 2,108 | 55 | 2001 | 8,956 | 363 |
| 1998 | 3,743 | 101 | | | |
| 1999 | 6,372 | 236 | | | |

2    You can look up the accounts of private limited companies at Companies House Information Centres. These are based in Birmingham, Cardiff, Edinburgh, Glasgow, Leeds, London and Manchester (for contact details see page 206). They all have computer access to the full records (held at Cardiff). Visiting is worthwhile, as the counter staff are very helpful. If too inconvenient or too expensive, phone to find out the latest charges, then write with your search request plus a cheque for the right sum. To look up a company in Companies House you need to know four things:

i   It only holds data for firms which have Ltd or plc after their company name.

ii  You will need to know the precise company name. This may sound obvious, but when you visit, you will learn that there are dozens of firms with similar names (but only one with the exact name of the company you are interested in).

iii At the start of 2001 each company search cost £5.00 (but £8.00 by post). If you apply by post, it is important to realise that the information will come on microfiche. This requires a microfiche reading machine (ask your local library).

iv  Before spending money in this way, it is important to realise that very small companies no longer have to declare their full accounts at Companies House. If a firm's annual turnover is below £2,800,000 and it has fewer than 50 employees, it only needs to supply abbreviated accounts. These are rarely worth having.

The other possible source of company accounts is Extel (now renamed Sequencer). Main libraries are likely to have this. It gives extracts from the accounts of thousands of private and public limited companies. It is easy to use, especially when available on CD-ROM. The list of libraries on pages 196 and 197 shows which libraries hold Sequencer.

| Project need | Source of information |
| --- | --- |
| The contact company's sales revenue and profit figures for the past five years (to provide background information) | For a plc, the latest annual report and accounts will provide the last five years' figures; for Ltd companies Companies House can provide the data |
| Details of the main shareholders of a Ltd company (to see if the managing director has the power to achieve the changes needed) | Companies House – look up on microfiche |
| The latest half-year or quarterly results for a plc (to update the annual report you already have) | Use Sequencer or the *Financial Times* CD-ROM, or www.ft.com (though your library will need to have a subscription) |
| Accounts for rival firms, for inter-firm comparison | Use Sequencer, Companies House or the *Financial Times Annual Report Service* |

# INTER-FIRM COMPARISON DATA

Dun & Bradstreet publishes an annual volume of financial ratios, *Key Financial Ratios*, which are a goldmine for project work. The book's strength is that its analysis of over 250,000 UK companies is broken down by sector. You can, therefore, find ratio analysis for book retailers, air-conditioning manufacturers or any other group among hundreds of analyses. This makes the format ideal for research assignments. If your project is on your aunt's bookshop, you can find out how her stock turnover compares with that of the average bookshop. Now analyse all her key operating ratios and you have the ideal preparation for deciding which aspects of the business need improvement.

The list below shows a few of the 370 business sectors analysed in *Key Financial Ratios*. The average stock turnover figure for the sector is given. This shows how wildly different the ratios can be and, by implication, how valuable it is to know the correct data relating to your business.

**Table 8.2**

| | Stock turnover – by industry sector |
|---|---|
| Retail chemists | 10.4 |
| Sports goods retailers | 3.7 |
| Record retailers | 4.6 |
| Petrol stations | 20.2 |
| Bread producers | 33.6 |
| Road builders | 23.9 |
| Residential building contractors | 2.8 |

Source: *Key Financial Ratios*, Dun & Bradstreet

## Projects in Practice

Joanna's business studies tutor put her in touch with a local small-scale producer of sports cars. She was given the accounts and other background data to help decide on her project title. She obtained the relevant pages of *Key Financial Ratios* (see page 57).

**Continued**

All the industry sectors are analysed in the same way as this information on motor vehicle manufacturers. The data is provided in three ways: upper quartile, median and lower quartile. Upper quartile shows the results for the best performing quarter of the firms in the sample. For the acid test ratio, for example, 0.9 was the average for the best 25% of the firms.

The median is a form of average – the middle figure within a range. Mean averages for the motor industry would be dominated by big firms such as Ford and Rover. The median is not, so it is more useful for Joanna's project.

Lower quartile shows the average for the worst performing quarter of the firms. For example, their return on capital averaged a 7.1% loss on every £ of capital employed.

Detailed analysis of the firm's accounts revealed one figure which seemed far out of line with the industry averages. The sports car company's debtor days figure of 86.3 was worse than the 67.6 day average for the lower quartile. Her project title became 'How can XXX Sports Cars improve its debtor days figure to the industry average of 45 days?'

**Table 8.3** Selected ratios from *Key Financial Ratios*, Dun and Bradstreet, published annually

| Motor vehicle manufacturers | Ratios by industry quartile | | |
| --- | --- | --- | --- |
| | **Upper** | **Median** | **Lower** |
| *Financial status* | | | |
| Acid test | 0.9 | 0.5 | 0.3 |
| Current ratio | 1.4 | 1.0 | 0.8 |
| *Asset utility* | | | |
| Stock turnover | 14.5 | 7.3 | 5.8 |
| Collection period (days) | 22.8 | 45.4 | 67.6 |
| Asset turnover | 2.86 | 1.99 | 1.31 |
| *Profitability* | | | |
| Profit margin (%) | 6.0 | 1.9 | (2.0) |
| Shareholders' Return (%) | 34.1 | 9.7 | (11.2) |
| Return on Capital (%) | 24.8 | 7.7 | (7.1) |
| *Ratios per employee (£000s)* | | | |
| Capital employed per employee | 33.7 | 12.6 | 2.0 |
| Sales per employee | 127.1 | 72.7 | 47.1 |

This inter-firm financial analysis is also extremely helpful for carrying out feasibility studies and business plans. This is dealt with in Chapter 17, which focuses on this type of project.

| Project need | Source of information |
| --- | --- |
| Setting a target for your contact company to achieve, such as a stock turnover of 15 times | upper quartile figures in *Key Financial Ratios* |
| Analysing the success of a new strategy by your contact firm, such as a move to JIT | assess the stock turnover trends among rival firms, by looking at several years of data in *Key Financial Ratios* |
| Judging the efficiency of your firm versus its rivals, e.g. in terms of sales per employee | the upper, median and lower figures in *Key Financial Ratios*, perhaps plotted on a bar chart, alongside your firm's data |

To show what your firm's balance sheet should look like, if your firm matched those in the upper quartile

upper quartile figures in *Key Financial Ratios*

---

Although *Key Financial Ratios* is a marvellous resource, it does have two drawbacks. The first is that the material is quite dated (about two years old by the time it is published). This does not have to matter. The stock turnover figures for all bookshops are unlikely to change much, year by year. As long as you make clear your reservations, the project examiner will accept that perfect comparisons cannot always be found in the real world. More important is the second drawback, that the book is very expensive and will therefore not be held in every library. The grid on pages 196 and 197 shows how few of the main libraries in the UK hold this information.

If your library does not have *Key Business Ratios*, an alternative is the similar *Industrial Performance Analysis* published by ICC Business Publications. This covers only 166 industry sectors but has the advantage of being slightly more up to date.

Regrettably, at the time of writing it is unclear whether Key Financial Ratios will continue to be published. Fortunately, as mentioned above, ratios change little over time (by sector) and therefore the data from 1998/99 (the last edition printed) will still be useful for several years.

## INFORMATION FROM PRESS MEDIA

This section can be divided into three: press cuttings, newspaper files/CD-ROMs, and the trade press.

Press cuttings services select, copy and make available articles from newspapers and magazines. Of particular value in business projects is a good press cuttings service focused upon company information. The best known of these is McCarthy's Information Service. Available at many libraries, this is a press cuttings service which provides an up to date file of articles on public (or major private) companies. Stored alphabetically by company, they are an easy way of obtaining background information. It is worth consulting such a source before visiting your contact firm for the first time (to impress those you meet) and to develop your project background later on. McCarthy's is available on paper cards, on CD-ROM and on-line. The libraries which stock McCarthy's are listed on pages 196 and 197.

Newspaper files and CD-ROMs can be almost as useful, though you have to do more to find what you need. The most valuable paper is likely to be the *Financial Times*, as it provides up to date, detailed information on latest company financial information. *The Times, The Guardian, The Independent* and *The Daily Telegraph* are also available on CD-ROM. In many cases these same resources are available on the Internet, but be careful to check on the cost of downloading/copying as it can be very expensive.

The trade press consists of magazines produced for people working within a particular industry or service. *The Grocer* is full of information on new products, services or opportunities within the grocery trade. Among the vast number of trade magazines are *Caravan Business, Confectioner, Tobacconist & Newsagent* and *Sandwich & Snack News*. Virtually every business sector has its own trade magazine. It can be hard to track down the relevant one, but a good starting point is *British Rate and Data* (BRAD), which is available in most public libraries with a reference section. Trade magazines can provide information such as:

- **up to date data on sales and investment within the sector**
- **case studies of relevant companies, often business start-ups**
- **names and addresses of suppliers to the industry (e.g. suppliers of shopfittings, cash tills and so on)**
- **articles on business issues of importance within the sector, such as franchising and factoring.**

A good example of the riches that can be found in trade magazines is the following table of information reported in *The Grocer*. Its detailed data on the confectionery market would provide the basis for an analysis of a newsagent's sales and stock levels, to decide whether it is stocking the right brands.

## INFORMATION FROM WEB SITES

There is so much information available that it is impossible to give general advice. In addition, the layout and content of sites change constantly. My main advice is:

- **get to know a good search engine really well ( I almost exclusively use www.google.co.uk and www.ft.com)**
- **don't overuse Internet-based information; it is usually rather out of date and often not quite what you want; libraries remain invaluable.**

**Table 8.4** Retail confectionery sales – all outlets (£000s)

| | Year to end Oct. 2001 | Year to end Oct. 2002 | % change |
|---|---|---|---|
| 1 Nestlé KitKat* | £116,924 | £96,018 | −17.9 |
| 2 Mars Bar | £120,935 | £110,547 | −8.6 |
| 3 Cadbury's Dairy Milk | £195,823 | £205,689 | 5.0 |
| 4 Mars Twix | £53,831 | £50,364 | −6.4 |
| 5 Mars Maltesers | £85,548 | £101,207 | 18.3 |
| 6 Cadbury's Roses | £66,211 | £67,624 | 2.1 |
| 7 Mars Celebrations | £78,028 | £73,943 | −5.2 |
| 8 Mars Snickers | £69,126 | £66,924 | −3.2 |
| 9 Nestlé Aero | £74,630 | £72,220 | −3.2 |
| 10 Nestlé Quality Street | £58,404 | £63,160 | 8.1 |
| 11 Mars Galaxy | £127,246 | £121,211 | −4.7 |
| 12 Mars Bounty | £43,748 | £40,430 | −7.6 |
| 13 Cadbury's Caramel | £30,257 | £41,597 | 37.5 |
| 14 Cadbury's Crunchie | £41,829 | £39,931 | −4.5 |
| 15 Cadbury's Fruit & Nut | £43,723 | £41,004 | −6.2 |
| 16 Cadbury's Milk Tray | £45,386 | £39,462 | −13.1 |
| 17 Cadbury's Creme Egg | £45,887 | £40,355 | −12.1 |
| 18 Nestlé Rolo | £25,860 | £34,356 | 32.9 |
| 19 Nestlé Smarties | £36,472 | £34,295 | −6.0 |
| 20 Cadbury's Whole Nut | £37,116 | £33,878 | −8.7 |
| Total market value | £1,422,844 | £1,374,215 | −3.5 |

Source: Information Resource, quoted in *The Grocer*, 14/12/02

*4-finger and KitKat Chunky only.

# Market research: effective primary research

## 9.1 Conducting a market research survey

About a half of all A level projects contain a market research survey. For those that do, it is often the technique that makes or breaks the assignment. Its importance is that it is often the crucial link between the project's aims and its conclusions. If conducted and analysed effectively, market research is the centrepiece of a project and the cement that holds it together.

Following the method outlined below should put your report head and shoulders above the majority.

## 9.2 Identify your research objectives

Any convincing survey is time consuming to devise, carry out and analyse. It can also be expensive, if carried out by post; you must therefore get it right first time. You cannot go back and add a question you forgot to ask.

The key to success is to be completely sure of your research objectives, in other words to know exactly what you want to find out. That may seem easy, even obvious, but it is very hard to do. After all, if you knew exactly what you wanted to find out, the whole project process would be quite straightforward.

To identify your objectives, ask yourself:

a   **Which aspects of my sub-objectives require primary research? (If you already have secondary data covering an issue, there may be no point in repeating it.)**

b   **What do I need to know to be able to tackle each sub-objective?**

c   **In what form do I need the information? (As a percentage of a large sample to help make a sales forecast or to provide some qualitative insights?)**

d   **What demographic (age, sex, income etc) information may be needed to analyse the findings?**

As a final check, think ahead to the conclusion you anticipate for your whole project. If, for instance, you are to recommend whether to proceed with a new product launch, do your research objectives include everything you need? Will you be able to forecast the sales, set the right price, choose the right advertising media and so on.

Once you have produced your research objectives, show them to your business contact and/or your tutor. It can also be very helpful to talk to one or two of those within your target population. For example, if you are surveying staff attitudes, a chat with an employee can quickly reveal a list of grievances you were unaware of. Discussion at this stage can save a great deal of time later on.

## 9.3  Decide on your methodology

### RESEARCH METHOD

Before you write the questionnaire you need to know how it will be used. If respondents are to fill it in themselves they will need very clear instructions throughout. So what is to be your research method?

Your options boil down to three:

1   a self-completion questionnaire

2   a telephone survey

3   face to face interviewing.

Wherever possible, you should go for the first option. It will be less time consuming and therefore enable you to get a bigger sample size. Unfortunately this approach is not always possible. Your sample must represent the target market you require. If your target is business people, 100 questionnaires filled in by students in your school/college library are irrelevant.

Self-completion requires you to have access to the right sort of people. The ideal is for them to be gathered together. For example, if your project is on a Chinese takeaway, nothing is easier than to get customers to fill in a questionnaire when they are waiting for their food. Alternatively, you may know the addresses of a company's clients, in which case a postal survey will be possible.

Unfortunately your target population is not always in the same place and you do not necessarily know their addresses, in which case face to face interviewing may be essential.

## Projects in Practice

Claire's assignment on forecasting attendance figures at Fulham Football Club included a survey of how other league and premiership clubs went about the task. Her sampling method was to select every second team from each division of each league. This ensured randomness, while, in effect, having a quota based on the right distribution of large and small clubs.

Her postal survey meant writing to 46 clubs (each addressed to 'The Commercial Director'). Along with the questionnaire she included a self-addressed envelope (not stamped, to save money). She received 26 replies – a very impressive response rate of over 50%. The results of the survey were so consistent that there was no reason to worry about the small sample size. Astonishingly, almost all the clubs guesstimate home attendances; only one had a computer model to carry out the task.

## SAMPLING METHOD

Sampling method needs to be considered at this stage because it may influence the way you construct your questionnaire. For example, if you are carrying out a quota or a stratified sample, your first question will be a screening one. If your sample is to be purely vegetarians, your first question must screen out meat eaters.

So which sampling method will you use? Random, quota, stratified or one of the less common ones, such as cluster or convenience, both of which are well suited to project work.

### Random sampling

Random samples are most likely to be used if you have access to a database or mailing list. From this you could select a sample on a random basis (such as every tenth name, or by making use of a random numbers table such as the one in appendix C). By this means, therefore, you could select 40 customers randomly from a database, then send a postal questionnaire to each.

## Quota sampling

Quota samples require you to know the profile of your target population. Then you can set out your target sample. For instance, you may be conducting a feasibility study into opening up a football café. Secondary sources such as Mintel would enable you to know the sex and age profile of football fans. You then set sample quotas as follows:

**Demographic profile of football fans**

| Demographics | Profile of football fans | Sample (size 40) |
| --- | --- | --- |
| Male | 75% | 30 |
| Female | 25% | 10 |
| 15–24 | 40% | 16 |
| 25–34 | 30% | 12 |
| 35+ | 30% | 12 |

This shows that 30 of the 40 interviews must be with men. It ensures that your sample is representative of the target population as a whole.

## Stratified sampling

This involves interviewing only one type of person, usually the type you see as having the greatest sales potential. For example, a project on 'Should the *Daily Express* relaunch itself to appeal to a new, younger market?' might carry out a survey of only 16–24-year-olds.

## Cluster sampling

Cluster samples are those gathered in only one or two localities. If your project has a national outlook, it would still be acceptable to only interview locally, using the rationale of the cluster sample.

## Convenience sampling

This is described by David Mercer in his book *New Marketing Practice* (Penguin 1997) as 'a polite phrase for interviewing whoever comes to hand'. It has no theoretical justification at all, but if it is the only practical way in which you can achieve a reasonable sample size for your research it can be justified.

# SAMPLE SIZE

Now is the time to consider the sample size you require. If the key aspect of your project is a sales forecast, carrying out research on 20 people would seem an absurdly small sample. So how big should it be? Many business decisions are made with samples of 120–200 people. Surveys can, however, have statistical validity with a sample size as low as 50.

It is important to remember, though, that in this case your project research does not have to be statistically valid. An excellent AQA project looked at the feasibility of opening up a tour operator specialising in fashion holidays (to see the Ralph Lauren autumn collections, for instance). The student sent a postal questionnaire to 25 travel agents. Twelve replied, each providing a great deal of insight into the problems this business would face. The sample size was too small for statistical validity, but in the circumstances it was wholly acceptable.

As a guideline:

- **If responses can be obtained quickly and cheaply (e.g. the Chinese takeaway, self-completion questionnaire) the sample size should be over 50**

- **If responses are expensive to obtain (postal questionnaires needing stamped addressed envelopes inside, or phone calls in business hours), at least 25 attempts should be made**

- **If responses are very difficult to obtain (face to face street interviews, for example), at least 10 is a fair target.**

## 9.4 Writing the questionnaire

Writing a questionnaire is time consuming and frustrating. More than any other aspect of the coursework, it is essential to word process your work. This is because you will need to keep re-drafting questions and juggling their order until you reach a satisfactory result. Professional market researchers expect to take a day to write a questionnaire, so do not expect to dash one off in an hour.

To write an effective questionnaire, bear in mind each of these points:

- **Beware of writing biased questions, e.g. 'How much do you like ...'.**

- **Avoid writing two questions in one, e.g. 'What do you think of the taste and texture of ...'**

- The meaning of each question must be crystal clear; you can only be certain of this by trying it out on a few people (known as piloting).

- The order in which the questions are asked is very important; ask yourself 'Do any of my questions pre-empt later ones?' The approximate order in which questions should be written is shown in the table opposite.

- If your sample is large enough, you may want to analyse the results through percentages and present them in bar charts; if so, closed questions will make your life much easier.

- Nevertheless the occasional use of an open question can be worthwhile, as it will generate comments which can enrich your report write-up (which otherwise can be too crammed with figures). Examples of open and closed questions are:

  *Closed question:*

| What did you think of your pizza? | Very good | _____ | Quite good | _____ |
| | Quite poor | _____ | Very poor | _____ |

  *Open question:*
  What did you think of your pizza?  _____

  _____

- The final (but most important) point is that you must make sure your questionnaire covers all your research objectives.

The table below sets out a fuller explanation of how to tackle a questionnaire. On the left is the instruction, on the right are practical examples of writing questions for a feasibility study into opening up a vegetarian café.

| Advice on writing a questionnaire | Question examples (for a feasibility study) |
| --- | --- |
| Write a brief introduction, which you must try to use the same way every time you begin an interview | Good morning/afternoon, I'm researching for an A level business studies project. May I ask you a few quick questions? |

Start with a general screening/warm-up question.

Do you ever eat meat nowadays?
Yes ___     No ___

Carry on with background questions, but make them more precise.

When did you last visit a vegetarian restaurant?
Within the last week ___
One to four weeks ago ___
More than four weeks ago ___
Never ___

It is very helpful to use the style of question opposite, which generates a great deal of information in tick-box form and can therefore be analysed easily.

When deciding to visit a vegetarian restaurant how important are each of the following?

| | importance: | | |
| --- | --- | --- | --- |
| | very | quite | not |
| Location | ___ | ___ | ___ |
| Food quality | ___ | ___ | ___ |
| Below £10 a head | ___ | ___ | ___ |
| Fast service | ___ | ___ | ___ |

Having obtained all the information you want (likes/dislikes, location, etc.) move to test your business proposition. Make sure to give as precise an explanation as possible. Respondents cannot be definite about a proposition they are unclear about.

I am thinking of opening a vegetarian café focusing on young people, offering cocktails, good music and good, snacky food. Would you:
definitely try it ___
be very likely to try it ___
probably try it ___
probably not try it ___
definitely not try it ___

Then follow this question up with an even more important one. Product trial is one thing; repeat purchase is everything.

Assuming you enjoy the food and atmosphere at the café, how often do you think you might visit?
once a month or less ___
two or three times a month ___
once a week ___
more than once a week ___

You might want further questions about location, price and opening hours before ...

A
B
C
D
E
F
G
H
I
J
K
L
M
N
O
P
Q
R
S
T
U
V
W
X
Y
Z

... finishing off with demographic information.

If possible leave this until last, because asking people's age and job can be regarded as prying. If they refuse to answer at the end, at least you've already completed the most important part of the interview.

Into which of these age groups do you fall?

| | | | |
|---|---|---|---|
| 15–24 | ____ | 45–54 | ____ |
| 25–34 | ____ | 55–64 | ____ |
| 35–44 | ____ | 65+ | ____ |
| Refused | ____ | | |

Are you in paid employment at the moment?

Yes ____

No ____

What is your job, exactly?

_____

Then sign off with thanks.

Thank you very much for your time.

For examples of successful project questionnaires, see the Appendix.

## 9.5 Conducting the survey

### RESPONSE RATE

Reliable market research requires not only a good questionnaire, an appropriate sampling method and a reasonably large sample size, it also requires a good response rate. If you post out 50 questionnaires and only five return, you have to ask yourself whether the five are likely to reflect accurately the views of the 50. Could it be that they are especially well disposed towards your idea or the firm you are working with? In which case your findings will be biased, through no apparent fault of your own.

You might, however, have been able to anticipate the problem. If you had sent stamped, addressed envelopes to 25 people, might you have ended up with ten responses?

A similar issue relates to self-completion questionnaires. You may leave them by a shop checkout, having asked the shop assistants to ask customers to fill them in. Might they ask their favourite/regular customers? Or might only the regulars bother? At the very least, make sure there is a method for counting the number of customers, so that you can include and comment on the response rate your survey achieved.

## AVOIDING FIELDWORK BIAS

If you go interviewing early on a Wednesday afternoon, you cannot expect a representative sample of people. So make sure that you spread your fieldwork over a realistic period of time. Ideally this should include a weekend day and perhaps an evening. Of course, this may not be possible, but if you cannot fulfil this rule, at least you could comment on it as a possible weakness in your method.

## 9.6 Analysing research results

If you have 50 completed questionnaires, each with 12 questions, you have a frightening mass of data. What is more, there are many different ways of analysing the information, so the permutations are seemingly endless. Some students feel the need to produce a bar or pie chart for every question they have asked; this is boring and offputting for the reader. It is far better to select the relevant data and exclude the rest.

## Here are some simple rules to follow in research analysis:

1   Go through each question, counting the responses. Are any of the results a surprise? Is the surprise of importance in relation to your project objectives? If so, it may form the centrepiece of your research analysis.

2   Having seen the results, consider which ones are helpful in answering key questions within your project. You will probably find that half your survey questions lead nowhere, in which case they can be set aside.

3   Convert the results for the more important questions into percentages, although if the sample size is less than 25, this is rather pointless.

4   Be sure to record the sample size for every question, especially when you convert the figures to percentages. There may be a question which is answered only by those who say 'no' to an earlier question. If you do not record the sample size, the examiner may wonder whether you realised the sample was only ten people. The quality of analysis you demonstrate depends upon your judgement of the reliability of the evidence you are using.

5   Most surveys have one or two questions which are the heart of the exercise. They enable a sales forecast to be made or an investment

appraisal to be undertaken. Concentrate a lot of your effort on these. Can the results be analysed further, perhaps broken down into the views of men and women, users and non-users or whatever else is appropriate? In-depth analysis of a crucial question will impress the reader far more than a superficial look at the whole questionnaire.

Students who enjoy figures may want to use a further method for analysing research findings. Called 'reweighting', it is explained in full in Chapter 11.

# How to analyse your findings

'Analysis' means: breaking down to identify the component parts and thereby discover the causes and effects of the parts coming together. For example, analysing a successful football team would require an assessment of each part of the team (defence, midfield, attack), followed by consideration of the manager's training methods, tactics and motivational talents, and finally a careful consideration of the causes and effects of the approaches adopted. To help in the process, it would be useful to have some statistical evidence, such as percentage of passes going astray, number of passes before the opposition touches the ball and so on.

As there are so many variables involved in football success, the analysis is helped if it is based on a theory. The most famous theory relating to football is that success comes from getting the ball forward as quickly as possible (the theory behind the 'long ball' game). An analyst could set out to measure whether Manchester United's success (at the time of writing) is due to the speed with which the ball gets to the opponent's penalty box.

Business projects are the same. The task of analysing your findings is to break down the information you have in order to explain the reasons behind a company's successes or problems. If possible, the next step is to find a theoretical model for measuring what is happening, why, and what can be done next. The table below provides a series of relevant examples.

| Project objective | Theoretical approach |
| --- | --- |
| To identify the cause of high labour turnover at XXX Ltd and recommend how to reduce it. | Use Herzberg's model of motivators and hygiene factors to analyse job satisfaction in the firm.* |
| To formulate a plan to restore XXX Engineering to profitability and thereby ensure its survival. | Use the Boston matrix to analyse the firm's eight main product lines in order to make pricing and marketing recommendations. |

| | |
|---|---|
| To undertake a feasibility study into opening a high performance gym. | Use investment appraisal to assess potential profitability. |
| To decide whether XXX Co. should move to a new, cheaper location. | Use breakeven analysis to measure the financial impact and critical path analysis to plan how to carry it out efficiently. |
| To decide whether DDD Co. should expand. | Use ratio analysis to investigate the current balance sheet and to estimate the impact on the company's finances of expansion. |
| To discover how YYY Grocers could improve staff morale. | Use Blake's grid to measure leadership styles among supervisors and managers.** |

*See the article in *Business Review*, February 1998
**See article in *Business Review*, September 1995

The reality of project work is often that you have gathered information from a variety of sources and are floundering in a sea of paper. Your first instinct is to write it up, but all this will do is provide factual content. How do you analyse the material? Attempt one or more of the following approaches:

- **Use a theoretical model (see above).**

- **Use a spider diagram approach to identify links between different pieces of evidence; later you may be able to present this as a flow chart, like the one shown below.**

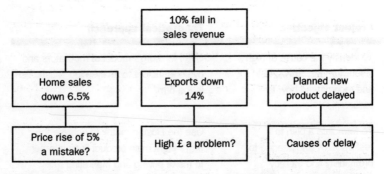

**Figure 10.1** Flowchart showing relationships and breaking the material down

- When working with data series, such as sales figures or absenteeism figures, do experiment with graphs to see whether any patterns emerge. For instance, it may be that you did not realise that the data had a seasonal pattern, absenteeism rising in the summer, perhaps. Spreadsheet computer packages are ideal for graphs based on trial and error, but if you have limited access to a computer, a few sheets of graph paper are all you need.

- When in doubt, ask. It is understandable if you become overwhelmed by the problem of analysing a great deal of data; ask your project contact for advice (but make sure you know the reasons behind the approach you are taking).

- SWOT analysis is often a helpful approach, that is analysing the strengths, weaknesses, opportunities and threats faced by the business you are looking at.

- An interesting alternative to a SWOT analysis is to conduct an audit, for example a human resources audit. In this case you would identify the firm's personnel needs and then compare the needs with what the firm has available (for example the firm may need one telephonist per shift who speaks French, yet only have one French speaker for two shifts).

There are many possible approaches to analysing project findings. The most important consideration, though, is that:

**Good projects are based on analysis targeted directly at the project objectives.**

Therefore the best way to pick through your findings is to identify what is relevant to each project objective, then organise your material accordingly. A good example is the presentation of market research findings. Many students use questionnaires to obtain primary data. The presentation of results forms the central section of many assignments. The reader often has to wade through page after page of graphs and explanations, a process which often ends up with the point of the survey being lost. The reader has become bored and confused.

Far better is to organise your findings into sections which relate directly to your objectives and methods. In other words, your findings section 4.3 relates to objective 2.3 and method 3.3. To tackle objective 2.3 you select the material which is relevant. This may include a section on market trends from a secondary research document, questions (5 and 8 perhaps) from your questionnaire and informal discussions with two of the firm's customers. You will in this way have used a variety of sources of data to achieve the project objective. This is well illustrated in the following example, especially section 2 on page 75.

## Projects in Practice

### Feasibility of opening a dance club in Croydon

#### Findings

Aim: to estimate the costs of setting up a new dance club in Croydon.

Method: interviews with two of the local nightclub owners; phoning suppliers as listed in the Clubs Directory; researching in the local paper and local estate agents for pay rates and property costs.

#### *Procedure and results*

*1 Building and related costs*

The average size of the venues in Croydon is 5,650 m$^2$. This provides a capacity of approximately 1300 people. The cost of purchasing such a site would be prohibitive (several £ million) therefore my plan would be to:

- rent a building shell with an option to buy
- employ an architect and obtain planning permission
- develop the site.

There are building regulations, health and safety aspects and the needs of local residents to be taken into account. I contacted an architect who informed me of the various aspects to consider. Based on his information and advice, I was able to estimate the following outlay within the first year:

- Planning permission: £1,200
- Building cost: £250,000
- Inspection fees: £3,500
- Building notice: £4,700
- Annual rent advance: £48,000
- TOTAL £307,400

**Continued**

In addition, licensing fees are necessary to obtain the public entertainment licence needed to operate a nightclub. This costs £100 from Croydon Council. So the total start-up cost of premises is: £307,500

## 2 Lighting

Although only 19% of club goers considered lighting to be important (see my questionnaire results in appendix C) the two club owners I interviewed regarded good lighting as vital to creating the right atmosphere. The Blue Orchid has a lighting rig consisting of 500 disco lights and 200 normal lights for just one of its four dance areas. Its total expenditure on lighting is said to have been £350,000. I think it important to create the best atmosphere of any club in town, so I plan to allow £450,000 for state-of-the-art lighting. This should give the club an edge over the competition and can be used as a unique selling point. So, lighting start-up cost is: £450,000

## 3 Bars

The two clubs which helped me in Croydon had an average of seven bars each. The main start-up costs are the tills, and industrial washing up machines. I was told that the display units, beer pumps and all the other fabric of the bars are provided free by the breweries, on the condition that they have a say over what is stocked. Glassware is replaced every month, and is made of a specially coated glass. The costs are:

- 8 washing-up machines at £400 each:        £3,200
- 30 boxes of beer glasses at £20 per box:    £600
- 30 boxes of other glasses at £40 per box:   £1,200
- TOTAL:                                      £5,000

## 4 Staffing

Staffing is a major element of the running costs of a nightclub. Of course these costs will be running costs rather than initial outlay, but you cannot run a club efficiently from its first day of opening unless the staff are fully trained to use the equipment. I am therefore going to budget for one month's staff costs within the

**Continued**

start-up costs, to give a full allowance for effective training.

The two clubs I visited had similar staffing structures. From these I have scheduled the following staffing pattern. In addition I have taken relevant wage rates from job advertisements in the local Croydon Advertiser:

| Type | Number | Wage rate | Monthly wage bill |
|------|--------|-----------|-------------------|
| Doormen | 8 | £300 per week | £9,600 |
| Cloakroom staff | 4 | £3.50 per hour | £1,008 |
| Bar staff | 21 | £4.00 per hour | £6,048 |
| DJs | 2 | £500 each per session* | £12,000 |
| Admission | 2 | £3.50 per hour | £504 |
| Other staff | 9 | various | £3,225 |
| TOTAL | 46 | | £32,385 |

*The rival clubs pay £150 per session, but I am intending to hire top Capital Radio DJs

In addition is the cost of uniforms, estimated at £5000.

Total for wages: £37,385

## 5 Other costs

Other start-up costs include a computer system linked to the tills to ensure efficient stock control (£60,000) and security systems such as closed circuit TV and closed circuit security radios (£9,000). The other key investment is a good sound system. The Blue Orchid told me that they are just about to replace their system for one costing £40,000. So I will take that figure as my own.

In addition, I think a £50,000 contingency allowance would be wise. This will provide for any unexpected costs.

Total other costs: £159,000

Continued

## *Summary of start-up costs:*

| Type | Cost | % of total outlay |
|------|------|-------------------|
| Building | £307,500 | 32% |
| Lighting | £450,000 | 47% |
| Bars | £5,000 | 1% |
| Staffing | £37,385 | 4% |
| Other costs | £109,000 | 11% |
| Contingency budget | £50,000 | 5% |
| TOTAL | £958,885 | 100% |

## *CONCLUSION*

From this objective I conclude that:

- an initial outlay of £958,885 will be required to set up the club
- the number of factors involved makes it desirable to use a planning technique such as critical path analysis to ensure that management effort is concentrated on the key success factors
- it is essential to get further practical details of how long it takes to obtain planning approval and to meet the regulations.

A B C D E F G H I J K L M N O P Q R S T U V W X Y Z

# Key forms of analysis for top grade projects

This section sets out a number of valuable forms of analysis. The options provide you with the ability to choose one that is relevant to your own project. It is hard to imagine any report containing more than two of these methods, and probably only one will be needed. It is also perfectly possible that none of the following may be relevant to the problem you are tackling.

The techniques covered are:

1 **sales forecasting for a new product/service**
2 **sales forecasting for an existing product/service**
3 **investment appraisal**
4 **correlation**
5 **analysis of capacity utilisation**
6 **reweighting**
7 **deflating to show real changes in revenue or costs.**

## 11.1 Sales forecasting (for a new product/service)

There are many possible ways to generate a sales forecast. Let us take for example the opening of a new branch of McDonald's.

### Method 1 Averaging the existing sales per outlet

The sales turnover of McDonald's UK Ltd is publicly available information, so is its number of restaurants, therefore its average UK turnover per store is easily accessible. If you had no access to any other sales forecast, this figure would do.

### Method 2 Forecasting sales in relation to sales at an existing outlet

Perhaps you work at the Doncaster McDonald's and are considering opening up a new outlet in Goldthorpe. Try to find out the annual sales turnover at your branch. Then go to your public library to find the populations of Doncaster and Goldthorpe. If Goldthorpe has two-thirds of the population of Doncaster, a sales forecast of Doncaster minus one-third would be fair. Though bear in mind that if Goldthorpe has special features (such as tourist attractions) the comparison may be misleading. In which case a traffic count might be helpful (counting the number of pedestrians passing the McDonald's at Doncaster to compare with the numbers at the site you propose in Goldthorpe).

## Method 3  Forecasting sales based on market research findings

When the business is a brand new idea there cannot be any directly comparable data, so market research results must be used. But how? You could do the following:

1   Conduct a survey of your target market, with a sample size of 50+.

2   Within it, ask a question such as:

At a price of XXp, would you buy this product regularly?

| | |
|---|---|
| Yes, definitely | ___ |
| Yes, very probably | ___ |
| Yes, possibly | ___ |
| Probably not | ___ |
| Definitely not | ___ |

3   Then apply the method used by American researchers known as the 90/30 rule. This states that you should take 90% of the 'definitely' category, 30% of the 'very probably' category and none of the other responses; from this you can work out an estimated market share. For example, if the responses to the above question were:

| | |
|---|---|
| Yes, definitely | 12% |
| Yes, very probably | 32% |
| Yes, possibly | 30% |
| Probably not | 18% |
| Definitely not | 8% |

the forecast market share would be:

| | | |
|---|---|---|
| $12\% \times 0.9$ | = | 10.8% |
| plus $32\% \times 0.3$ | = | 9.6% |
| Total | = | 20.4% |

4    Find the market size locally (e.g. the local 15–34-year-old population can be found at your local library). Then apply the market share percentage. For instance, if there are 3600 15–34-year-olds in the town, your forecast is: 3600 × 20.4% = 734 customers.

5    To complete the sales forecast you need to be able to multiply this figure by the number of times customers are likely to buy per year and also by the intended selling price, both of which can be found through your questionnaire, or perhaps from secondary sources.

## Projects in Practice

Kamal's project was on opening up a video hire shop for business customers (training videos etc.) in Bristol. He decided his target market was Bristol firms with at least ten employees. The local chamber of commerce told him there were approximately 1200 of these. He sent a postal questionnaire to 90, 44 of which were returned. These 44 gave him the following results to the questions he asked:

**Q1**  Are training videos ever used within your business?
Yes: 34 (77%)    No: 10 (23%)

**Q4**  I am considering setting up a video store in the city centre specialising in training videos for businesses. There would be a viewing facility, for you or your staff to check whether the video meets your needs. We would also deliver and collect the videos anywhere in the Bristol postal district. Rental cost would be between £60 and £120 per day.

Do you think your firm might use this service on a regular basis?

| | |
|---|---|
| Yes, definitely | 32% |
| Yes, very probably | 25% |
| Yes, possibly | 13% |
| Probably not | 18% |
| Definitely not | 12% |

**Q5**  For those who say 'Yes, definitely' or 'Yes, very probably' ask:

**a**  For how long do you think you would hire a training video:
One day only                    58%

---

**Continued**

| | |
|---|---|
| Two days | 27% |
| Three days | 12% |
| More than three days | 3% (The average is 1.6 days) |

**b** How many times per year might you hire a training video?

| | |
|---|---|
| Once only | 43% |
| Two-three times | 31% |
| Four-five times | 18% |
| Six or more times | 8% (average 2.5 times) |

---

All this information allowed Kamal to produce the following estimate of his annual sales revenue:

---

**Continued**

## 1 Forecast number of customers

Total market size: 1200 firms minus the 23% who do not use videos = 924 firms

Market share (Q4, applying the 90/30 rule)

| | | |
|---|---|---|
| 32% × 90% | = | 28.8% |
| + 25% × 30% | = | 7.5% |
| | = | 36.3% |

Number of customers: 924 firms × 36.3% = 335 customers

## 2 Forecast revenue per customer

£90 average daily rental × 1.6 days × 2.5 times per year = £360 per year

## 3 Forecast annual sales revenue

335 customers × £360 = £120,600

## 11.2 Forecasting sales on an existing product

The key to a good project is to look to the future. That is what all business decision making is about. Therefore projects should always be looking ahead to next year's sales/plans/problems, not last year's.

One of the most common research assignments sees a student attempting to improve the profitability of a struggling firm. The student analyses the workings of the business, then suggests improvements. The test of success will be the predicted effects on profitability of the recommendations. This process can be enriched hugely if the report begins with a forecast of what is likely to happen if no changes occur (see Figure 11.1). Such a forecast can be used as the yardstick for judging the value of the student's recommendations. At the heart of this process is the sales forecast.

## Projects in Practice

My project is based upon the difficult sales position faced by my uncle's bicycle business. Sales have been drifting down over the past two years and I forecast that this downturn will continue.

**Actual and Forecast Sales of XXX Ltd.**

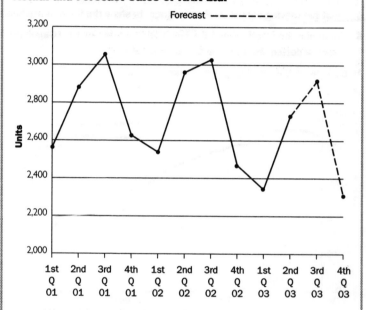

**Figure 11.1**

I intend to focus upon the objective of seeing how the business could restore sales in the 4th quarter of 2003 to the level of the same quarter in 2001.

There are four main ways of forecasting the sales of an existing product or service. All are based upon extrapolation, that is, predicting the future based upon past trends. Most require you to obtain monthly sales figures for at least the past three years.

## Method 1  Extrapolation based on a moving annual total

1   Take the first 12 months' data and add them up (e.g. March 2000–February 2001).

2   Take the next 12 monthly period (in this case April 2000–March 2001).

3   Carry on for as long as you can (i.e. up to the latest month's data you have available).

4   Plot the moving annual totals on a graph to show the trend in the data.

5   Continue the trend beyond the last relevant data point (extrapolation) using a dotted line to show it is an estimate.

An example of the resulting graph is shown below.

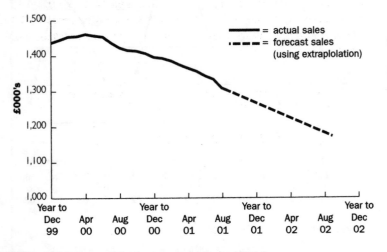

**Figure 11.2** Extrapolation based on moving annual total

## Method 2  Extrapolation based on moving monthly averages

1   Take the first 12 months' data (e.g. March 2000–February 2001). Add them up and divide by 12 to give a monthly average.

2   Take the next 12 monthly period (in this case April 2000–March 2001) and repeat the exercise.

**3** Carry on for as long as you can, up to the latest month's data you have available.

**4** Plot the moving monthly averages on a graph to show the trend in the data.

**5** Continue the trend forward (extrapolation) using a dotted line to show it is an estimate.

## Method 3 Extrapolation based on seasonally adjusted monthly figures

This method is far more complicated and fiddly. Its great strength, though, is that it enables you not only to forecast future trends, but also individual monthly figures. This is valuable if there is a strong seasonal pattern to demand. For example, if your project title is 'Should the BDZ Co. expand its production capacity?' a key issue is to show if or when output reaches full capacity. As the figure below shows, this may require monthly figures, not annual trends.

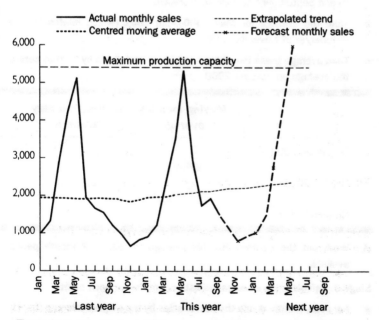

**Figure 11.3** Extrapolation based on seasonally adjusted monthly figures

The method starts in the same way as the moving monthly averages:

*Stage 1  Calculate moving monthly averages*

a  Take the first 12 months' data (e.g. March 2000–February 2001) add them up and divide by 12 to give a monthly average.

b  Take the next 12 monthly period (April 2000–March 2001) and repeat the exercise.

c  Carry on for as long as you can, up to the latest month's data you have available.

*Stage 2  Centre the moving averages*

This makes them comparable with actual monthly data. The problem is that when 12 months' data is averaged, the average relates to halfway through the 12 month period. If you think about it, you will reach halfway through a year at the end of June/beginning of July. So which month does the year's average relate to, June or July? To solve this problem, you centre the average on the middle of the months.

a  Take the average for the period April 2000–March 2001 (which relates to end September/start October 2000).

b  Take the average for May 2000–April 2001 (which relates to end October/start November 2000).

c  Then average these two figures (add both and divide by two) to centre the average on October 2000.

|  | Moving monthly average | Centred monthly average |
|---|---|---|
| September 2000 | | |
| | £28,400 | |
| October 2000 | | £29,500 |
| | £30,600 | |
| November 2000 | | |

d  Work out the centred monthly average for each 12 month period available.

*Stage 3  Calculate the seasonal adjustment factor for each month*

a  For every month, divide the actual sales by the centred average (trend) figure.

**b** This shows the proportion of the trend level achieved each month. For example, in the table below, actual sales in October were 1.25 times the trend level. January's were well below the trend.

| Month | Actual sales that month | Centred trend figure | Seasonal variation |
|---|---|---|---|
| October 2000 | £36,875 | £29,500 | 1.25 |
| January 2001 | £24,800 | £31,800 | 0.78 |

**c** Take the seasonal variations for the same month of each year for which you have data, then average them thus:

October 1999    1.18 ⎫
October 2000    1.25 ⎬ average = 1.23
October 2001    1.26 ⎭

**d** In this case the October seasonal adjustment factor is therefore 1.23.

*Stage 4 Extrapolate the centred monthly (trend) data forward to cover the future period you require*

**a** Plot the past trend data on a graph.

**b** Extrapolate the line forward, distinguishing future from past by making the forecast a dotted line.

*Stage 5 Estimate future sales per month*

**a** Read the forecast trend data off the graph.

**b** Apply the seasonal adjustment factors to forecast sales for specific months.

**c** Plot the forecast monthly figures on a graph as shown in the graph for Method 3.

## Method 4 Projecting forward based upon annual figures

If you are unable to obtain monthly data, you may have to rely on annual sales and/or profit figures. You could extrapolate the figures forwards, by plotting the data on a graph and extending the line of best fit. This method is less impressive, mathematically, than the previous three. So why not consider adjusting this forecast in line with other information, some of which may be qualitative? For instance a business owner might say 'All the papers are predicting a recession. The last time that happened we did pretty well.' In which case it would be fair to edge your forecast above the extrapolated level.

## 11.3 Investment appraisal

This should need no introduction as it is a standard part of the A level syllabus. It is possible, though, that you have been taught the calculation element of appraisal without understanding where the figures come from. When carrying out research assignments understanding is the key aspect.

Take, for example, the standard presentation of appraisal data:

|  | Cash in | Cash out | Net cash flow |
|---|---|---|---|
| Year 0 | – | £42,000 | (£42,000) |
| Year 1 | £60,000 | £40,000 | £20,000 |
| Year 2 | £80,000 | £48,000 | £32,000 |
| Year 3 | £80,000 | £48,000 | £32,000 |
| Year 4 | £55,000 | £40,000 | £15,000 |

The top class project is one which explains exactly how the cash inflows were estimated (perhaps by using the sales forecasting technique outlined on page 78), then justifies fully the initial cash outlay and the ongoing cash outflows. The secret is to provide explanatory notes, perhaps cross-referenced to fuller detail on another page. So a far better presentation than the above is:

|  | Cash in | Notes/sources of information |
|---|---|---|
| Year 0 | – | |
| Year 1 | £60,000 | Price £4 × 15,000 units (see sales forecast) |
| Year 2 | £80,000 | £4 × 20,000 (see sales forecast) |
| Year 3 | £80,000 | £4 × 20,000 (forecast) |
| Year 4 | £55,000 | £4 × 13,750 (forecast) |

| | Cash out | Notes/sources of information |
|---|---|---|
| Year 0 | £42,000 | Initial outlay |
| Year 1 | £40,000 | £24,000 direct costs + £16,000 overheads |
| Year 2 | £48,000 | £32,000 of direct costs + £16,000 overheads |
| Year 3 | £48,000 | £32,000 of direct costs + £16,000 overheads |
| Year 4 | £40,000 | £22,000 of direct costs + £18,000 overheads |

| | Net cash flow | Notes/sources of information |
|---|---|---|
| Year 0 | (£42,000) | Payments on the initial outlay spread over three months |
| Year 1 | £20,000 | Slow sales build-up means weak cash flow in first half |
| Year 2 | £32,000 | Cash flow spread evenly across the year |
| Year 3 | £32,000 | Cash flow spread evenly across the year |
| Year 4 | £15,000 | Sales falling away pushes cash flow down |

Before moving from this data to appraisal methods such as payback and net present value, it is very effective to provide a graph of the cash flows. This illustrates the financing needs. For example, the figure overleaf shows the above data, but with the added assumption that the firm has £30,000 of its own capital. The graph then indicates clearly the finance gap which would need to be tackled by negotiating an overdraft, for example. Your project might show the finance gap in red, to help the reader follow your argument.

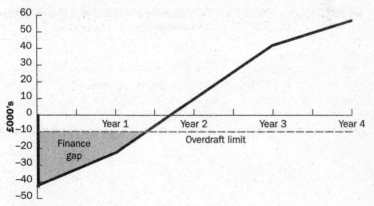

**Figure 11.4** Net cash flows on an investment

## 11.4 Correlation

Correlation means identifying relationships between series of numerical data. An example might be finding out how sales of iced lollies vary when the temperature changes. This can lead to some useful project analysis with a practical benefit to your contact firm. It can also help you make recommendations, such as that a shop selling ice cream should base its summer ordering on the weather forecast, anticipating demand instead of waiting for stocks to run low.

Correlation can be carried out very simply using scatter graphs. These have the twin benefit of being easy to do and impressive to see. With iced lollies, for example, you could record sales per weekday at your contact shop over a period of ten days in August. At the same time, record the temperature per day as shown in the following day's local newspaper.

|  | Week 1 | | Week 2 | |
|---|---|---|---|---|
|  | Temperature | Sales | Temperature | Sales |
| Monday | 24° | 22 | 19° | 8 |
| Tuesday | 27° | 33 | 24° | 19 |
| Wednesday | 22° | 16 | 27° | 31 |
| Thursday | 20° | 11 | 29° | 40 |
| Friday | 20° | 13 | 28° | 38 |

This data can then be plotted on a scatter graph and the line of best fit identified as shown below. The line of best fit can then be turned into a ready-reckoner for the shop owner, showing, for example, that if tomorrow is forecast to be 26°, 30 lollies will be needed.

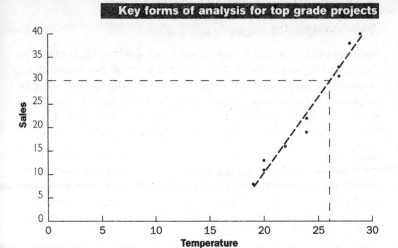

**Figure 11.5** Scatter graph showing correlation between lolly sales and the weather

## Projects in Practice

Claire Marston undertook a research assignment titled 'Would Fulham Football Club benefit from changing its method for forecasting home attendance?' The heart of the project was to be her attempt to produce a formula for modelling home attendances. She set out with the assumption that the key variables would include:

- current league position
- recent results
- Saturday or midweek match
- league position of opponent
- average home attendance of opponent.

She succeeded in finding a correlation between these (and other) variables and was therefore able to provide a model predicting attendances. The club regarded the information gained as confidential, therefore the detailed results cannot be provided.

Claire's project then went on to analyse the business benefits of her forecasting method. These included the effects on programme ordering, staff scheduling (turnstile operators, stewards, programme sellers, etc.) and catering supplies.

## 11.5 Analysis of capacity utilisation

Many firms suffer from low average capacity utilisation. This causes high fixed costs per unit, which cut into the profit margin. Often the reason for low average utilisation is time based. Demand may be seasonal or may fluctuate within the week or the day. The table below sets out a few examples of each type.

| Seasonal fluctuations | Day to day fluctuations | Hour to hour fluctuations |
| --- | --- | --- |
| air-conditioning | cinema/snooker club | restaurant/pub |
| toy producer/shop | restaurant | leisure centre |
| garden centre | baker | taxi/mini-cab |
| off licence, jewellers or any other gift shop | clothes shop | dry cleaner or photo processor (if near station) |

Projects on businesses like these can make a central feature of the analysis of capacity utilisation. Having analysed utilisation with care, the report can focus on strategies for improving demand in off-peak periods. This might require methods such as promotional pricing or product/service diversification.

Generating the necessary data on utilisation can be time consuming. It may be achieved by sifting through the organisation's records, such as till receipts, production schedules or weekly sales records. Often, though, it requires observation. As you will rarely be able to observe for long enough time periods, it may be sensible to set up a recording system which staff are asked to fill in for a week or two. For example, at a dry-cleaners there could be a sheet of paper such as that shown below. This can then be converted into a graph as illustrated.

**Utilisation Record at Dry Cleaners: Thursday 24th June**

| Time period | Customer bringing clothes in | Customer picking up completed order | Other customer contact |
|---|---|---|---|
| 8.00–8.29 | JHT | I | I |
| 8.30–8.59 | JHT JHT III | JHT I | III |
| 9.00–9.29 | JHT JHT I | III | II |
| 9.30–9.59 | JHT I | IIII | III |
| 10.00–10.59 | JHT | JHT | IIII |
| 11.00–11.59 | IIII | JHT I | IIII |
| 12.00–12.29 | JHT I | JHT | III |
| 12.30–12.59 | JHT III | JHT IIII | JHT |
| 1.00–1.29 | IIII | JHT II | IIII |
| 1.30–1.59 | IIII | JHT III | III |
| 2.00–2.59 | III | JHT | I |
| 3.00–3.59 | I | III | |
| 4.00–4.59 | JHT | JHT III | II |
| 5.00–5.59 | II | JHT III | IIII |
| Total | 77 | 78 | 39 |

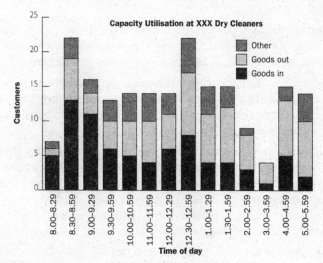

**Figure 11.6** Time/business pattern for a dry cleaners

## Projects in Practice

Tracey Clarke worked at a leisure centre which was struggling to meet the financial targets set by the local council. She looked into the costs of running the centre, deciding that there was little scope for cutbacks. She decided that improving utilisation was a good way to boost income at minimal marginal cost.

She used the centre's booking sheets to construct detailed records of the usage of squash courts, gym, fitness centre and badminton courts. These showed that the squash courts had the greatest imbalance between daytime and evening demand (during weekdays). Tracey ended up recommending a mailshot to local school PE teachers, offering a special school rate for block-booking the courts. Her report concluded with a letter from the centre's manager thanking her for her work and stating that Tracey's suggestions would be put into practice the following September.

## 11.6 Reweighting

### A STATISTICAL INTERLUDE – HOW TO REWEIGHT SAMPLE FINDINGS

This next section should only be read by those who love numbers. It puts forward a technique which is very useful, but very fiddly. If your assignment is short of detailed analysis, this method could be a useful way of generating marks.

Reweighting is useful if you know that your sample was unrepresentative of your target population. This happens most often when students 'top-up' their samples by asking fellow students. This means the age category 16–18 becomes over-represented.

For instance, a student assignment on opening an Indian wedding clothes shop involved a survey. The sample proved heavily weighted towards teenagers. To make it more representative, the student found out the marriage age profile of Indian women in the UK and reweighted the survey data to bring it into line. In other words, because teenagers were over-represented, their views were given less influence within the sample findings.

The figures below show how to do this. Note that the 'Yes' response is 23 out of 50.

| | | Student's survey data | | | |
|---|---|---|---|---|---|
| | | All | 15–20 | 21–29 | 30–39 | 40+ |
| Would you travel to | Yes | 23 | 8 | 9 | 3 | 3 |
| Leicester to visit | No | 27 | 17 | 6 | 2 | 2 |
| a wedding clothes | | | | | | |
| shop? | | | | | | |
| | Total sample | 50 | 25 | 15 | 5 | 5 |

| Age | The student's sample profile | Actual profile | Implied weights* |
|---|---|---|---|
| 15–20 | 50% | 25% | 0.5 |
| 21–29 | 30% | 45% | 1.5 |
| 30–39 | 10% | 20% | 2.0 |
| 40+ | 10% | 10% | 1.0 |

*These figures show what needs to be done to the sample data to bring it into line with the known actual (secondary) data, that is to halve the value of the 15–20 group responses, multiply the 21–29 group by 1.5 and so on.

Data reweighted to allow for sampling inaccuracies:

| Age | Sample findings | Weight | Weighted result |
|---|---|---|---|
| 15–24 | 8 | 0.5 | 4.0 |
| 25–34 | 9 | 1.5 | 13.5 |
| 35–44 | 3 | 2.0 | 6.0 |
| 45+ | 3 | 1.0 | 3.0 |
| | | Yes total = | 26.5 |
| | | = | 53% |

To summarise:

| | Yes | No |
|---|---|---|
| Unweighted results | 46% | 54% |
| Reweighted results | 53% | 47% |

So reweighting the sample findings produced a different (and more accurate) result.

## 11.7 Deflating data to show real changes in revenue or costs

Many small firms go from year to year without making much financial progress. Last year's £50,000 turnover becomes this year's £50,800. Next year it may slip back to £49,000. Often one finds that the proprietors are unworried by this. This is partly because, as long as profits are high enough to keep the family fed and holidayed there is no pressure. It is also because of an unhealthy tendency to ignore inflation in the calculations.

If inflation is 4% per year, last year's £50,000 needs to become £52,000 this year and £54,080 next. Over a few years this may not matter, but in the longer term it will make a huge difference to the firm's ability to keep the family in comfort, to keep the business equipment up to date, and indeed to survive at all.

So, when you obtain data showing the revenue and profits of a small firm over the past five or ten years (as you should, to help provide the reader with the background to the firm) consider the impact of inflation upon the figures.

A good way of doing this is to deflate the data by stripping inflation out of the figures. In the example given above, the firm's annual turnover figures need 4% inflation taken out. Because inflation compounds on itself, this is not quite as simple as deducting 4% for the first year and 8% for the second. The correct calculations are as follows:

|  | Sales turnover | Inflation index | Divide by index figure $\times$ **100** | Real turnover (at last year's prices) |
|---|---|---|---|---|
| Last year | £50,000 | 100 | Not applicable | £50,000 |
| This year | £50,800 | 104 | £50,800/104 × 100 | £48,846 |
| Next year | £49,000 | 108.16 | £49,000/108.16 × 100 | £45,303 |

The deflated figures on the right are telling the real story. This firm's revenues are falling fast – in terms of what they will buy given rising prices. With a few more years of information to show an even starker pattern of decline, this kind of information can make an excellent graph. (See the Projects in Practice example below.)

## Projects in Practice

Josh's parents own and run a dry-cleaning business. They are reasonably happy with the way it has been performing and would like their son to look at possible ways of expanding in the future. Josh identifies two possibilities: opening a second outlet or diversifying to attract company business (such as cleaning company uniforms). After some prompting, he produces the following data for the background section of his assignment.

| Year | Sales turnover |
|------|----------------|
| 1993 | £22,600 |
| 1994 | £24,700 |
| 1995 | £24,600 |
| 1996 | £23,800 |
| 1997 | £22,100 |
| 1998 | £22,700 |
| 1999 | £23,000 |
| 2000 | £23,500 |
| 2001 | £24,600 |
| 2002 | £25,900 |

This can be turned into a rather dull graph, but when the figures are deflated by the Retail Price Index (the main measurement of inflation in the UK) the data look far more interesting (and worrying).

| Year turnover | Sales turnover | RPI (reweighted to 1993) | Sales in 1993 |
|---------------|----------------|--------------------------|---------------|
| 1993 | £22,600 | 100 | £22,600 |
| 1994 | £24,700 | 107.5 | £22,977 |
| 1995 | £24,600 | 118.1 | £20,830 |
| 1996 | £23,800 | 125.0 | £19,040 |
| 1997 | £22,100 | 131.8 | £16,768 |
| 1998 | £22,700 | 136.6 | £16,618 |
| 1999 | £23,000 | 142.1 | £16,186 |
| 2000 | £23,500 | 149.1 | £15,761 |
| 2001 | £24,600 | 152.9 | £16,089 |
| 2002 | £25,900 | 157.5 | £16,444 |

Continued

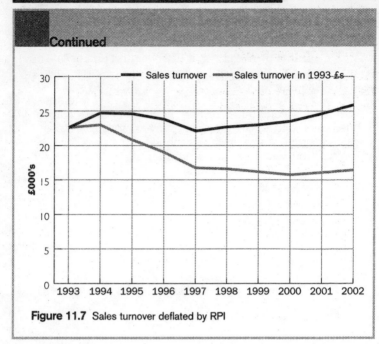

**Figure 11.7** Sales turnover deflated by RPI

# ✓ Checklist 3
## Am I progressing?

These are the tasks you should tackle in the second half of the project process. They should be completed two months before your deadline for project completion. Use the checklist to review your progress.

| | Yes | Partly | No |
|---|---|---|---|
| **1** Has effective secondary research been completed into: | | | |
| The market background | ☐ | ☐ | ☐ |
| The company background | ☐ | ☐ | ☐ |
| Consumer usage and attitudes | ☐ | ☐ | ☐ |
| AND HAVE THE RESULTS BEEN ANALYSED? | ☐ | ☐ | ☐ |
| **2** Has effective primary research been conducted on: | | | |
| (N.B. probably only one of the following.) | | | |
| Staff | ☐ | ☐ | ☐ |
| Customers or potential customers | ☐ | ☐ | ☐ |
| Suppliers | ☐ | ☐ | ☐ |
| Distributors/retailers | ☐ | ☐ | ☐ |
| AND HAVE THE RESULTS BEEN ANALYSED? | ☐ | ☐ | ☐ |
| **3** Has this research been related directly to your project objectives? | | | |
| Objective 1 | ☐ | ☐ | ☐ |
| Objective 2 | ☐ | ☐ | ☐ |
| Objective 3 | ☐ | ☐ | ☐ |
| Objective 4 | ☐ | ☐ | ☐ |
| Objective 5 | ☐ | ☐ | ☐ |
| **4** Have the findings been discussed with: | | | |
| Teacher/tutor | ☐ | ☐ | ☐ |
| Contact/company | ☐ | ☐ | ☐ |

A B C D E F G H I J K L M N O P Q R S T U V W X Y Z

# Writing conclusions

It is hard to provide general rules on writing a conclusion. This is because a good conclusion emerges from the report's analysis and from the lessons learned by you, its author. To illustrate this, two very different A level project conclusions are reproduced later in the chapter. For now, here are a few general points.

## 12.1 Give yourself enough time

The exam skills assessed primarily in the conclusions to projects (synthesis and evaluation), can amount to as much as 40% of the total coursework marks. Therefore anyone leaving the conclusions until the day of the project deadline is a fool (I have at least a couple of students who do this each year).

To make sure of a high score for a conclusion it is probably wise to leave a week to plan and write it, discuss it with others and then edit into its finished form. As the following points will make clear, there is no shortage of things to cover, only shortage of time in which to cover them successfully.

## 12.2 Separate recommendations from conclusions

Every project should contain recommendations. After all, what is the point of a business investigation without positive suggestions on future action? Even comparisons between firms should include recommendations on how the weaker firm should act to catch up with the stronger one. If recommendations are included within general reflections on the assignment, they lose their force, so keep them separate.

## 12.3 Recommendations

Recommendations should be in the form of numbered points, with full justification of every point. It will often be helpful to relate each recommendation to the relevant objective. To maximise its impact, each recommendation should be costed and have a timescale as follows:

**Objective:** to cut labour turnover

**Recommendation:** to increase paid holidays from 4 to 6 weeks for those with 2–4 years' service

**Justification:** research showed dissatisfaction with holiday time among this high-turnover group (see p.21 for full details)

**Cost:** £50,000 in a full year, based on £250 × 2 weeks × 100 staff

**Timescale:** put to next board meeting, for implementation in January next year.

Note that it will often be appropriate to refer back to earlier sections of your project.

To make a good recommendations section great, discuss each recommendation with a relevant person. A feasibility study could be discussed with a bank manager or small business advisor from the bank. A problem solving project within a business could be talked over with your contact.

It is important to remember here that your project grade will be affected little by whether you have made the 'right' recommendations. So do not steal your contact's thoughts and present them as your own. If your contact's views are very different from the recommendations you have made, never mind. Record the contact's thoughts, then analyse them as part of your conclusions. Whether you own up to an error or argue vigorously for what you believe, extra marks await you.

## Projects in Practice

### (This is Kelly's 'Final recommendations' section)

My objective was to improve the cash flow position in order to eliminate the firm's £50,000 overdraft

## Recommendation 1: Factoring

- I recommend the factor Alex Lawrie whose services should be obtained through Lloyd's Bank.
- I recommend non-recourse factoring, which is when the factor takes on the responsibility for the debt. XXX Ltd. qualifies for this service as its annual turnover is above £250,000.

The effect of this recommendation will be to provide a cash injection of £39,000 (see section 3.3).

### Recommendation 2

To change the supplier payment system from end of the month to end of the following month. This will improve cash flow by one month of supplier payments (£15,000).

### Recommendation 3

To hold a half day conference for staff to explain the importance of cash flow, what affects it and the purpose of the changes (cost: £1800).

### Recommendation 4

To write to all suppliers explaining the new policy and the reasons for it (cost: £400).

| Recommendation | Effect on cash flow | Timing |
|---|---|---|
| 1  Factoring | +£39,000 | Negotiations should start now |
| 2  Delay supplier payments | +£15,000 | six weeks from now |
| 3  Staff conference | −£1,800 | three weeks from now |
| 4  Letter to suppliers | −£400 | four weeks from now |
| Net effect of recommendations | = +£51,800 | |

If these recommendations are followed, the objective of eliminating the overdraft will have been realised.

## 12.4 Conclusions

There are likely to be two main parts to a project conclusion: conclusions regarding the business and personal conclusions/reflections on the whole exercise.

## Conclusions regarding the business

When you started your assignment you probably knew very little about the firm, its internal workings and its marketplace. By the end you know far, far more. Perhaps you now know that the issue you tackled was not as important as you thought. It may even have been quite beside the point. Many past projects started off tackling an issue such as staff retention, appraisal or health and safety, only to find later that the key problem was of managerial attitudes. Now is the time to reflect on what you have learned in general about the business. What underlying issue(s) did you uncover? Does the business seem capable of managing and financing its ambitions? Are there weaknesses or threats it seems to be ignoring? And, though this strays towards the next section, what project do you now think you *should* have done?

The other aspect to business conclusions is that they should draw appropriately from your recommendations. If your proposal is that a sole trader should open a second shop, make sure to point out the new demands on the proprietor's time and managerial skills. What new qualities will be required? Has the proprietor got those qualities (or the relevant experience)? In other words, your conclusion might be that although the proposal looks financially sound, you doubt the entrepreneur's ability to make it a success.

The following example shows no hesitation in making recommendations which are supported by concluding comments such as 'I feel it would be a waste of resources to offer more variety unless we were prepared to match ...' This is also a good approach.

### Projects in Practice

How can XXX department store in Croydon improve its profitability to match its other branches in the region?

On the basis of the evidence I have gathered the Croydon branch can improve its profitability by:

1 Phasing out the cosmetics department, and using the floor space to extend concessions and multiples. This recommendation is based on my findings in section 5.2 which suggest that clothes have more earning potential than cosmetics. My analysis showed that cosmetics generates only 5.5% of revenue, compared with 12.4%

**Continued**

by multiples and 20.1% by concessions. The results of my questionnaire suggest that the reason for the poor performance by the cosmetics department is its unpopularity with customers.

As clothing has more profit potential than cosmetics, I recommend the firm capitalises on this asset in order to improve profit. I feel that extending concessions and multiples will push the branch's profit figures towards those of the average for the region.

2 The questionnaire highlighted that customers were unhappy with the range of cosmetics on offer. However I would not recommend the branch to improve the variety of cosmetics, as I feel this would not boost turnover and profits overall. My analysis of local competition showed that Allders had an extremely extensive cosmetics department. I feel it would be a waste of resources to offer more variety unless we were prepared to match the huge display at Allders, and I cannot believe that would be economic.

## Personal conclusions about the project process

So, how was it for you? Time consuming, infuriating, frustrating, confusing, depressing, unsettling, frantic. Yes, yes, but apart from that?

Among the huge list of issues you might consider are:

- **the skills it has helped you acquire, such as researching, IT (especially word processing and spreadsheets), structuring and editing a report**

- **the lessons it has taught you about your weaknesses, such as poor time management and lack of planning and initiative**

- **lessons about your strengths, such as (let's hope) good organisation, good interpersonal skills (conversational, in particular) and commitment to high standards**

- **the key role of objectives; without them, effort lacks focus and therefore can be wasted**

- **the need to ask for help, rather than 'keeping your head down' when things are tricky**

- **the value of evidence and the difficulty of obtaining it**

- **the extent to which business studies has been brought to life (however painfully) by the assignment**

- **the extent to which the project helped you learn techniques which previously were mysteries (e.g. investment appraisal)**

- **the extent to which the project gave you a better understanding of the integrated nature of the subject (how the departmental functions fit together)**

- **the extent to which the project gave you a feel for the uncertainty involved in every business decision, due to the number of questionable assumptions which have to be made**

- **how much there is to admire in successful entrepreneurship; high profits become more acceptable when the level of risk is understood**

- **the questionable way in which business decisions are rooted in figures (often suspect), leaving qualitative or moral factors to be treated as an afterthought.**

Of course, no one could or should tackle all these issues. Within the list though, there may be two or three which strike a chord in you. If so, aim to write a full paragraph (around 100 words) on each.

## Projects in Practice

(Matthew wrote the following, in a final conclusion to his feasibility study into opening a nightclub.)

This project has taught me a large (and frightening!) amount about myself. I have also learnt a lot about the complexity of constructing a business plan. The main conclusions I have drawn are:

- Time management is an important skill that I have learnt a lot about. I started this project in June of my first year, yet found time running out the following March. The need to plan research accurately and

**Continued**

effectively was an important aspect of the project. For each objective a variety of information had to be obtained in order to construct the relevant financial documents. I learnt a lot about the need to organise and plan my time effectively and feel such skills will assist me in further education.

- I feel the project aided me in the development of my communication skills. Carrying out a feasibility study meant the need to arrange interviews and carry out questionnaires. All these involved communication with a wide variety of people and the communication of the objectives I was trying to achieve. They also aided in the development of my self-confidence. I feel that the project helped me to learn self motivation. Due to the timespan of the project, we students were left to our own devices. This meant we needed to motivate ourselves and plan the work on our own.

- Revision was another area that was helped by this project. I had to look back over my notes to refresh my memory on some key business techniques. It also helped to identify the areas of the course I was weak at, acting as a key tool in planning my revision.

- From this study I also learned a large amount about the level of uncertainty that arises in business decision making. When constructing this project I learned just how many variables need to be considered when looking at the financial feasibility. Many of these factors are hard to predict, and variations would have a large effect on the final conclusions drawn. Many assumptions have to be made, and many of these are based on uncertain information. Hence the actual result is likely to turn out differently. The fascination of the subject is that one cannot know in which direction the inaccuracies will occur!

# Design, communication and illustration

Good projects look good. They look as though someone has taken the time and care to present their findings in the best way available. They do not need to be high tech or full colour masterpieces of IT. They do need to look well planned and carefully carried through. So what are the key features of a well set out project?

Most important by far is that the layout should help the reader. There are various ways in which you can do this.

## 13.1  When typing/printing

Your project has to be written up as a business report. The key feature of a report is that different managers might dip into different parts of it. The marketing manager might only be interested in the results of a customer survey, whereas the managing director might only read the recommendations. Consequently the report must be structured so that people can find their way around it. Headings must be clear; there must be a contents page and each section must be numbered so that it is easy to refer the reader forwards or backwards.

For instance, if your recommendations (on p.34, say) were largely based on research findings you had explained on p.22, you would tell the reader, 'As outlined on p.22, paragraph 4.3 ...' The key, therefore, is to number your paragraphs. By implication, you cannot expect a busy managing director (or examiner) to have to read the whole of p.22 to find the part you are referring to. So number your paragraphs.

Most businesses use the following approach:

1   **Main sections, e.g. Background: 1.0.**
2   **Main sub-sections, e.g. Background to company: 1.2.**
3   **Paragraphs within sub-sections, e.g. paragraph 4 of Background to company: 1.2.4.**

This approach can be seen clearly in the report layout shown on the next page.

15) **Investment Appraisal**
- **15.1 Reasons for Choosing Investment Appraisal Techniques**
- **15.2 Estimating Demand for the Future**
- **15.3 Pay Back Period**
- **15.4 Internal Rate of Return**
- **15.5 Sensitivity Analysis**
- **15.6 Summary**

## 15.1 Reasons for Choosing Investment Appraisal Techniques
The investment appraisal techniques that I have chosen to assess the viability of opening up an Asian boutique are:

**Pay Back Period**
This is a method of investment appraisal that estimates the length of time it takes to recoup the cash outlay on an investment. The reason I have chosen this method is because it will give me an indication as to when it will get my money back and from this I can estimate the risk of the investment.

---

*The advantages of Pay Back*
**Theory**
- Useful to firms with cash flow difficulties, as it helps to identify how long it will take for the cash to be restored.
- Since pay back only focuses on the short term (the period until the money is paid back) it is less likely to be inaccurate.

*The disadvantages of Pay Back*
- This method focuses on time but ignores profit, making it of limited use
- It may encourage a short termism.

---

**Internal Rate of Return**
Internal Rate of Return is the discount rate which, when applied to a net cash flow make their net present value zero. This can now be compared to the current rate of interest. If the IRR is higher the project is attractive.

## 15.2 Estimating Demand for the Future
On page 28 is a detailed cash flow forecast for year 1. To continue my forecast into the future I need to estimate demand trends. From the graph on page 2 (Background Research), I extended the line of Asian population increases from 1992–1996 to the year 2000. From this I got the following results.

| Year | Asian Adult Population | Index 1992 = Base year 100 |
|------|------------------------|-----------------------------|
| 1996 | 1125 | 100 |
| | *Forecast Asian Adult Population* | |
| 1997 | 1162 | 103.3 |
| 1998 | 1198 | 106.5 |
| 1999 | 1212 | 107.8 |
| 2000 | 1241 | 110.3 |

**Figure 13.1**

These additional points are also important to bear in mind:

* **make the font size large enough to be readable; 10 point is a bit small, but more than 13 point looks silly, so 11 or 12 point are ideal**

* **keep the line length short enough to make the writing easy to follow; approximately 13 words to a line seems about right; this will mean keeping quite wide margins**

* **keep paragraphs relatively short; your writing style should be businesslike and therefore concise; I have seen a project with a whole page of uninterrupted text and no paragraph breaks; who could read this and understand it?**

* **allow plenty of space between paragraphs and sections; students could often improve the look of their work greatly by using more blank lines.**

## 13.2 Using tables and figures

Tables such as sales data or labour turnover figures can provide important evidence to support your arguments or recommendations. If so, make sure they are properly presented. The best way is to make the information small enough to allow a full commentary to accompany the figures. Then the reader is clear about the particular conclusions you draw from the information. As shown in the extract that forms Figure 13.2, some students fill whole pages with numbers. This inclines the reader/examiner to turn the page over, looking for some analysis or judgement about the data and in so doing the whole point of a lengthily gathered table of data may be lost. The same problem arises if important figures are put into an appendix; the busy reader tends not to bother to refer to the information.

So, with tables of data:

* **limit the volume of information, to keep it manageable**

* **keep each table small and neat, within a page of text**

* **refer on that page to the key findings and conclusions**

* **consider using a highlighter pen to link your text/commentary to the relevant figures**

* **always state the source of the information.**

Exactly the same advice is relevant to figures such as a copy of a firm's balance sheet or profit and loss account; here, though, it may be unrealistic to

**Trend in sales and seasonal variation of H.J. Johnson Ltd**.

| Year | Sales | 4Q Total | C. Trend | Moving average | S. variation |
|------|-------|----------|----------|----------------|--------------|
| '90 Q1 | 34778 | | | | |
| '90 Q2 | 38100 | | | | |
| | | | 178761 | | |
| '90 Q3 | 31730 | | | 182530 | 45632.5 | 0.6953 |
| | | | 186299 | | |
| '90 Q4 | 74153 | 178761 | | 193171.5 | 48292.875 | 1.5355 |
| | | | 200044 | | |
| '91 Q1 | 42316 | 186299 | | 211319.5 | 52829.875 | 0.801 |
| | | | 222595 | | |
| '91 Q2 | 51845 | 200044 | | 225335 | 56333.75 | 0.9203 |
| | | | 228075 | | |
| '91 Q3 | 54281 | 222595 | | 227446 | 56861.5 | 0.9546 |
| | | | 226817 | | |
| '91 Q4 | 79633 | 228075 | | 232505.5 | 58126.375 | 1.37 |
| | | | 238194 | | |
| '92 Q1 | 41058 | 226817 | | 241113.5 | 60278.375 | 0.6811 |
| | | | 244033 | | |
| '92 Q2 | 63222 | 238194 | | 230633.5 | 57658.375 | 1.0965 |
| | | | 217234 | | |
| '92 Q3 | 60120 | 244033 | | 217330 | 54332.5 | 1.1065 |
| | | | 217426 | | |
| '92 Q4 | 52834 | 217234 | | 207658.5 | 51914.625 | 1.0177 |
| | | | 197891 | | |
| '93 Q1 | 41250 | 217426 | | 193601 | 48400.25 | 0.8523 |
| | | | 189311 | | |
| '93 Q2 | 43687 | 197891 | | 192105.5 | 48026.375 | 0.9096 |
| | | | 194900 | | |
| '93 Q3 | 51540 | 189311 | | 196150 | 49037.5 | 1.051 |
| | | | 197400 | | |
| '93 Q4 | 58423 | 194900 | | 194406.5 | 48601.625 | 1.2021 |
| | | | 191413 | | |
| '94 Q1 | 43750 | 197400 | | 183088 | 45772 | 0.9558 |
| | | | 174763 | | |
| '94 Q2 | 37700 | 191413 | | 181865.5 | 45466.375 | 0.8292 |
| | | | 188968 | | |
| '94 Q3 | 34890 | 174763 | | | | |
| '94 Q4 | 72628 | 188968 | | | | |

**Q1 Total**  $0.801 + 0.6811 + 0.8523 + 0.9558 = 3.2902$
$3.2902 / 4 = 0.8226$

**Q2 Total**  $0.9203 + 1.0965 + 0.9096 + 0.8292 = 3.7556$
$3.7556 / 4 = 0.9389$

**Q3 Total**  $0.6953 + 0.9546 + 1.1065 + 1.051 = 3.8074$
$3.8074 / 4 = 0.9519$

**Q4 Total**  $1.5355 + 1.37 + 1.0177 + 1.2021 = 5.1253$
$5.1253 / 4 = 1.2813$

**Figure 13.2**

miniaturise the information. Balance sheets are complex enough without making the figures unreadably small. In such cases there are two ways to keep the data full page size while still being able to write a commentary alongside:

1 **Photocopy the full page of data onto the back of the previous page. Then the reader can see the data on the left with your written commentary on the right-hand page. If photocopying is difficult, pasting the data to the back of the previous right-hand page achieves the same effect (though less tidily).**

2 **Sellotape the data to the commentary page, so that the reader flaps it out to the right of the text.**

## 13.3 Presenting data

Some computer games use graphs and tables superbly. When you have just achieved a great score, they tell you so, allowing you to see yourself in the 'All time top 10', or analysing your performance. Other games have graphic overload, showing so many ways of looking at your performance that you are unsure: first what they mean and secondly which are the most important measurements.

Projects can be the same. Having been told of the importance of graphical presentation of data, some students go crazy. They produce graph after graph, of market research findings, financial performance, sales figures and anything else they can think of! Selectivity is vital.

The skill of selectivity can be shown in three main ways:

1 **Choose which information to illustrate. Just because you have obtained some data does not mean it is relevant to meeting your coursework objectives; your final report should include only relevant data even if that means scrapping masses of figures and graphs.**

2 **Decide which type of graph to use (line graph, pie chart, bar chart, etc.); the principles here are very clear. For changes over time, use line graphs or vertical bar charts; for showing the composition of data (40% men, 60% women etc.), use pie charts or bar charts (usually horizontal ones work better).**

3 **Choose the prominence to give to each graph. If you have found out some crucial information make sure to present it prominently. Perhaps make it your only colour graph or produce the graph on a double page which the reader has to flap open.**

### The dos and don'ts of project graphs

### Project dos

☑ Be clear about the project objective the graph is intended to help you meet, and make it clear to the reader.

☑ Provide enough information on the graph to make it interesting. Usually, a single line on a graph looks feeble; is there nothing to compare the data to? If you are showing a firm's sales over recent years, can they not be compared with profits, or trends in the market as a whole?

☑ When making comparisons between data of different sizes, consider indexing. For example, the BMV Co.'s sales and profit figures would generate the graph shown below. The indexed data is shown in the second graph (see Fig 13.4). Notice how much more analytic potential there is with the indexed graph.

BMV Co. – Sales and profit trends 1996–2001

|  | 1996 | 1997 | 1998 | 1999 | 2000 | 2001 |
|---|---|---|---|---|---|---|
| Sales turnover (£000s) | 142 | 156 | 184 | 208 | 214 | 216 |
| Profit (£000s) | 26 | 38 | 47 | 50 | 42 | 35 |
| Sales index (1996 = 100) | 100 | 110 | 130 | 146 | 151 | 152 |
| Profit index (1996 = 100) | 100 | 146 | 181 | 192 | 162 | 135 |

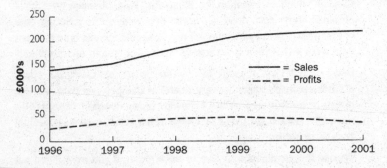

**Figure 13.3** BMV Co's sales and profits

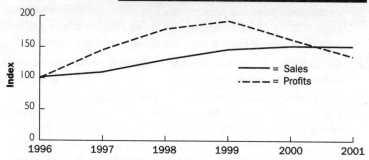

**Figure 13.4** BMV's indexed sales and profits

**4** An alternative to indexing is to use different scales on the left and right sides of the graph. For example, sales in thousands of pounds on the left and profits in hundreds of pounds on the right. This enables comparisons to be made while also enabling the reader to see money values (which are hidden by indexing). The figure below uses the same data from the BMV Co. to show this approach.

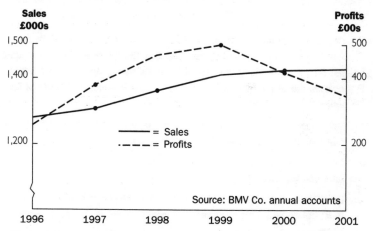

**Figure 13.5** How different scales can be used on either side of a graph

**5** Take care to label your graphs in great detail, including the source of the information.

**6** Make your graphs small enough to include on a page of text. Then your written explanation can help the reader understand the points you are trying to make, as in paragraph 4, above.

7    If you have a particular point you want to make about one part of the graph it is useful to either point to it (as here) or to use coloured highlighter pens to make a clear link between text and visual.

8    Be inventive. A student of mine wanted to show the capacity utilisation of squash courts at a sports club. She was keen to demonstrate that Saturday and Sunday usage patterns were different to each other, and to weekdays. But putting all three lines on a graph made the information hard to follow: it looked a mess. Her solution was to draw a graph with only the weekday utilisation. She then drew Saturday's data on a transparent sheet and taped it to the right-hand edge of the graph (positioning it carefully). The sheet could be lifted up (to see weekday only) or put down, to compare weekdays with Saturday. She repeated the process with Sunday, then wrote a note for the reader. This suggested starting by looking at the weekday pattern, then steadily adding the weekend days to get a clear understanding of the different usage patterns. It was highly commended by the examiner.

## Don't:

1    Don't use technology for the sake of it. Three-dimensional graphs rarely help and often hinder understanding. See the figure at the end of this list for an particularly poor graph. Hand drawn graphs using different colours are often clearer than those computer generated in black and white.

2    Don't ignore the virtue of a simple table of numbers. Sometimes the numbers are clearer than the graph they can create.

3    Don't put too much on a graph. Lots and lots of differently coloured bars can be baffling. As ever, be selective.

4    Don't lose sight of your objectives. A diagram is only worthwhile if it helps you communicate relevant findings to your reader/ examiner.

## 13.4  Using summaries

The reader of a 20–30 page report can struggle at times. Concentration can lapse, especially when the subject matter is a little dry. Even if concentration is high, the topic may be so complex that the arguments are hard to follow,

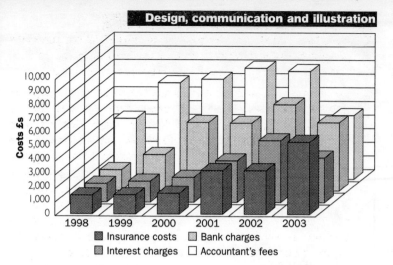

**Figure 13.6** This graph contains too much confusing information

in which case the examiner may be less than generous in awarding marks for communication.

A simple way round this is to provide summaries. At the end of each section of your report provide a summary of your key findings and/or conclusions. This shows what you judge to be the key factors (potential evaluation marks) and gives the reader an easy way to refer back to earlier passages within the assignment.

## 13.5 Glossary, bibliography and acknowledgements

Most projects include a bibliography and acknowledgements. Glossaries are rarer, but at least as important. Each of these features is explained in detail in the A–Z section of this book.

Another feature which would be worth considering is a letter from your contact. Nothing impresses an examiner more than evidence that the student's efforts have helped the contact company. So if your contacts have been able to learn something from your research or have been helped to think through a problem, ask if they would be kind enough to write a brief letter to that effect. Headed company letter paper and a bit of praise can go a long way. (Obviously, if the contact is a relative, this does not apply.)

## Checklist 4
### Am I finished?

These are the questions you must ask before you complete your project report. You should be considering them while you still have time to fill any gaps – two to three weeks before the final deadline. Use the checklist to review your progress.

|  | Yes | Partly | No |
|---|---|---|---|
| **1** Have the findings: | | | |
| Addressed every project objective in turn? | ☐ | ☐ | ☐ |
| Been analysed quantitatively and qualitatively | ☐ | ☐ | ☐ |
| Been presented relevantly and interestingly | ☐ | ☐ | ☐ |
| **2** Are the recommendations: | | | |
| Clearly focused on the project objectives | ☐ | ☐ | ☐ |
| Costed and given a recommended timescale | ☐ | ☐ | ☐ |
| Justified by evidence and argument | ☐ | ☐ | ☐ |
| Summarised, to show how they relate to the objectives | ☐ | ☐ | ☐ |
| **3** Have the project conclusions: | | | |
| Assessed the project implications for the business | ☐ | ☐ | ☐ |
| Been discussed with the project contact | ☐ | ☐ | ☐ |
| Discussed what you have learned from the work | ☐ | ☐ | ☐ |

continued

# Checklist 4 – continued
## Am I finished?

4  Have you made sure to:

State sources of information,
including a bibliography ☐ ☐ ☐

Provide a glossary of key
industry jargon (if needed) ☐ ☐ ☐

Provide brief summaries of
your sections/arguments ☐ ☐ ☐

Number pages and include
a contents page ☐ ☐ ☐

A B C D E F G H I J K L M N O P Q R S T U V W X Y Z

# The AQA project

This section sets out what you need to know to get a high grade on the AQA project. It is written on the assumption that you have already read Chapters 1–13 of this book.

The AQA project has several distinctive features:

1  **a choice between one of eight prescribed titles, or an independent study of a business problem or opportunity identified by you**

2  **a target word length of approximately 3000 words**

3  **fully explained marking criteria, which place heavy emphasis on synthesis and evaluation**

4  **internally assessed, but externally moderated.**

Each of the features is more fully explained in Sections 14.1–14.4. The AQA syllabus points out that, 'candidates must complete one project, either chosen from the range of specified projects or one of their own choosing. Each involves primary research, either within a specific organisation or via a survey of consumers or retailers. The research focus should usually be local rather than national.'

## 14.1 Your choice between the different types of AQA project

### TYPE A  CHOICE BETWEEN THE EIGHT AQA PROJECT TITLES

#### A1  Starting up a business

This is a feasibility study into the financial viability of a new business opportunity. It is one of the most frequently conducted projects and can generate excellent grades. It requires independent primary and secondary research to assess whether a new business proposition is financially viable. Sample titles include:

1   A feasibility study into opening a specialist music retailer in Altrincham High Street.

2   Should Mr Humphreys open a bicycle repair shop in Scarborough?

3   An investigation into the financial viability of opening a new cyber-café.

Feasibility studies are explained fully in Chapter 17. They are usually seen as a fall-back position, enabling a student with no business contact to produce a well-researched but independent assignment. Yet some teachers encourage all their students to carry out feasibility studies because they believe they offer greater scope for top marks. Whether this is true or not is unclear, but it suggests that you should not reject the idea of a feasibility study, even if you have a good contact within a business.

In the case of the above titles, the third was carried out by a student whose uncle was making a good living out of a chain of cyber/internet cafes. Instead of working within the business, she chose to use his cost data to make her own business start-up exercise more accurate. She reflected afterwards that 'It gave me the freedom to work on things my own way, asking for specific information if I needed it. Otherwise I would have ended up doing what my uncle told me to do, which would have been very irritating.' Her project received a B grade.

Useful academic starting points for this project include:

*Budget start ups* (100 ways to start a new business on £10,000 or less); McBennett R., Management Books, 2000.

*The E-commerce Book*, Korper S. and Ellis J., Academic Press, 2001.

## A2   A case study of a reorganisation

This studies the reorganisation of operations within a manufacturing or service business. This will usually look at a reshuffle that has already taken place, analysing its causes, the way it was carried out and its effects.

Candidates could consider:

* **the reasons behind the reorganisation (e.g. reduction in market share)**
* **the objectives behind the policy**
* **the plan for reorganisation**
* **the effects on the company**

- **any resistance to change**
- **the effectiveness of internal communications through a staff questionnaire (this may require company vetting/approval)**
- **any lessons learnt by management**
- **the success (or otherwise) of the process.**

With any project that looks back at an event there is a risk of the report becoming descriptive. 'The company did this, then did that ... The staff were apprehensive, but now prefer the new system ...' It is therefore important to identify ways to generate analysis and evaluation.

Analysis can best be achieved by ensuring that you have several sources of information. A single contact can only give his or her version of events. You can do no more than repeat it, giving little scope for analysis or insight. With two or three different versions of the same events, you have a great deal more to think and write about. Why do the versions differ so wildly, even over 'facts'? Is there any reason to suppose that one version is more independent and unbiased than the others? If so, why? Obtaining several views can enhance marks for methodology and also give plenty of scope for analysis and evaluation.

A different way to analyse the events within a reorganisation is to take an academic approach. What do business writers and experts suggest is the 'right' way for managers to handle a change such as this? And how does the company's approach compare with the theory? This method ensures a strong potential for analysis marks and lays the ground work for effective evaluation within your conclusions.

As reorganisations occur so frequently in modern businesses, this project title should provide scope for thinking ahead, and deciding which lessons you believe the company *has* drawn from the process as opposed to the lessons you believe they *should* have learnt.

Useful academic starting points for this project include:

*Organisational Behaviour and Analysis*, Rollinson D. *et al.*, FT, Prentice Hall, 1998 (especially Chapter 19 on Organisational Change).

*The New Corporate Cultures*, Deal T. & Kennedy A., Texere Publishing, 1999 (especially Chapter 3 on Downsizing and Reengineering).

Delayering Tactics, April 1997, *Business Review* by Boaz J.

# A3 A study of the effect on business(es) of a local development

This looks at the effect on local firms of a significant external change such as a new shopping centre, a major factory opening or closing, the establishment of a red route or the pedestrianisation of a town centre.

This project could work well, even if you start with no business contacts. To be successful, however, you will need to carry out effective qualitative and quantitative research among local firms and/or local people and/or local pressure groups. Gaining different viewpoints will be essential. If this is only achieved through secondary sources, such as the local newspaper, the validity of the research method will be undermined.

An unwritten rule of projects is that easy tasks require complex methods and hard tasks require easy methods. This project is potentially very easy to complete, so beware of underestimating it. Unless you have spoken personally to the different interest groups, it is likely that the project will be descriptive. Fortunately the topic does provide scope for a high grade, as long as you are able to discuss seriously the actual or potential impact of the development upon local businesses you have interviewed personally. Often, this will need to be separated into the short-term effect (usually negative) and the longer term impact. Try wherever possible to discover evidence such as forecast and/or actual effects upon sales turnover, upon profits, upon staff and upon firms' medium to long term plans.

Candidates could consider:

- **the development and its timescale**
- **the local issues as raised by the local media, and prepare a brief review of these**
- **the likely impact upon one or two local firms; following discussions with them candidates should write a questionnaire based on these discussions**
- **the findings from a postal or face-to-face survey of 10–15 local firms, used to gain their opinion of the actual (or potential) effect they expect to suffer**
- **the influence of external factors upon firms, and draw conclusions.**

Useful academic starting points for this project include:

*Harvard Business Review and the Environment*, Harvard Business School Press 2000, (especially Chapter 2, Bringing The Environment Down To Earth).

*Managing Sensitive Projects*, D'Herbemont O. & Cesar B., Macmillan, 1998 (quite academic, containing many valuable lines of thought).

## A4  An advertising project

Candidates should decide upon a new product which they believe would be popular (based upon discussion of market segmentation, product innovation and consumer trends). Ideally the product should be in an existing, large marketplace for which plenty of secondary data exists (such as soft drinks or confectionery). Candidates could consider:

- **the product idea, its niche and its rationale**

- **the market background: market size, market growth, competitors, consumer characteristics (age, sex, region, etc.), distribution outlets plus forecasts of the future, as can be found in secondary sources such as Mintel, Consumer Goods UK or Key Notes, see Chapter 8 for a thorough account of what is available and note the website addresses listed on pages 190–193**

- **the market positioning, potential consumer resistance and type of advertising needed (persuasive? informative?) from an analysis of the data**

- **the potential of the idea; decide upon a suitable price and determine which media are watched/read/listened to by those who expressed interest in purchasing, based on evidence collected via a quantitative survey on a sample of at least 50 school/college students**

- **which media to use, then cost out a suitable campaign using *British Rate and Data* (BRAD) to find the cost of the advertising proposed. (BRAD is available at most public libraries)**

- **whether it is worth proceeding with the idea, draw conclusions and make a fully justified recommendation.**

This project offers scope for a great deal of secondary research. It carries the risk that you will provide too much data that you have merely gathered from sources such as *Key Notes*. If you have done little to analyse the material, you cannot expect good marks. Therefore the key is to use data selectively, making sure to identify interesting ways to analyse the material. Chapter 11 of this book may help.

Successful advertising projects tend to hinge upon the plausibility of the new product idea. Only if the idea is believable are you likely to feel committed to thinking the whole exercise through. So do spend some time coming up with something fresh. In 1992 I read a student project on a robot vacuum cleaner. It seemed radical and new, but plausible. James Dyson launched just such a cleaner in 2002.

To achieve good marks for evaluation, it would be very helpful to get a professional to look at what you have produced. So if you have family or school/college contacts with a marketing professional, ask that person to read your finished report and discuss its strengths and weaknesses. This will provide plenty of scope for an excellent concluding section.

Useful academic starting points for this project include:

*The Fundamentals of Advertising*, 2nd Edition, Wilmshurst J. & Mackay A., Butterworth Heinemann, 1999 (especially Chapter 3, 'How Advertising Happens').

*Effective marketing*, Hingston P.; Dorling Kindersley, 2001 (especially section 1, 'Planning your marketing').

## A5 A case study of an entrepreneur

This forms a study of the motivations, aptitudes and achievements of the proprietor of a business that has started up within the past five years. The topic provides scope for a thorough examination of business theory. Do business start-ups really use cash flow forecasts and break-even analysis based upon carefully constructed sales forecasts? Is it a planned, scientific process or are the motives rather personal and the methods rather amateurish?

By making comparisons between business theory and reality, it should be possible to conduct effective analysis. Given the context, such analysis should span written and numerical techniques. As an example of the latter, it would be great if the proprietor still had a copy of the original business plan. Comparing actual cash flow and profit against the forecast level would generate excellent scope for analysis and evaluation.

Despite the great scope for a top-grade project, bear in mind that success will depend upon the entrepreneur's willingness to provide facts and figures. This is particularly important if there is no possibility of obtaining a range of views upon the start-up process. This is less of an issue if there are people who were there at the start and who can now comment and criticise from a different perspective. Such people may include bank managers, accountants, any staff employed from the start or – perhaps most revealingly – the entrepreneur's spouse, children or other family members. A period remembered by the entrepreneur as thrilling may be recalled by the family as stressful and unpleasant.

Candidates could consider:

* **the business(es), its market and its competitors**
* **the context and process of the business start-up**
* **the proprietor's motivations through motivation theory**
* **the extent to which the entrepreneur uses business methods such as cash flow forecasting and break-even analysis**
* **the future of the business through a survey of its customers**
* **the survey findings in relation to other evidence**
* **the role and the rewards of being an entrepreneur.**

Useful academic starting points for this project include:

*Entrepreneurs: Talent, Temperament, Technique*, Bolton B. & Thompson, J.; Butterworth-Heinemann, 2000 (especially Chapter 1, 'Identifying the Entrepreneur').

*Entrtepreneurship and Small Business,* Burns P.; Polgrave Press, 2001 (especially Chapter 2, 'Heroes and Superheroes').

*Amazon.com*, Spector R.; Random House, 2000 (provides a full case study on Jeff Bezos, founder of Amazon.com).


## A6  A SWOT analysis of a small to medium-sized manufacturer

This is a report based on a factory visit and talks/presentations from any two of the following senior personnel: Chief Executive/Managing Director; Works Director/Manager; Sales/Marketing Director/Manager. Talks could involve the whole class and are best conducted at the workplace.

Candidates should consider:

* **the brief history of the firm and the reasons for its current location**
* **the firm's main products, markets and competition; turnover trends (and profit, if possible) for the last five years**
* **the firm's main strengths ...**

- – ... **weaknesses** ...
- – ... **opportunities** ...
- – ... **threats**

  **each from the differing perspectives of the two speakers, and including every aspect of the business, as well as the candidate's perceptions when looking around the plant**

- • **the conclusions drawn: surprising? predictable? open to questions? attractive place to work? why?**

Of all the coursework suggestions for AQA, this has the most scope for ending up as a weak, descriptive report. You will need to be especially careful to think of lines of analysis that enable you to bring theory to bear. Before going it would be useful to read about Michael Porter's 'five forces' model for analysing the external environment within which businesses work. Alternatively, you might plan to analyse the firm through such methods as: Ansoff's matrix; the Boston matrix; the impact of seasonality upon revenues and operations, or determine to obtain actual stock figures on a key item, to compare actual data with the straight lines drawn on textbook stock control graphs.

Plan your analytic approach in advance so that you have done the required reading and therefore know which questions to ask of the experts you are meeting. Having gathered data from the firm, it may be valuable to compare some of the firm's performance indicators against those available in Benchmark Index, a government sponsored booklet that provides some data on indicators such as the acid test ratio (average 1.0) and training expenditure per employee (average £111 per year).

Useful academic starting points for this project include:

*Benchmark Index*, the Benchmark Journal, managed on behalf of the DTI by Winning Moves Ltd., Lea House, Station Road, Barlaston, Stoke-on-Trent, Staffs, ST12 9DA. Website: www.benchmarkindex.com.

*Operations Management*, 2nd edition, Slack N. *et al.*, FT Prentice Hall, 1998 (excellent reference source for theory on JIT, capacity utilisation, stock and quality control etc).

# A7 Study of a firm's personnel performance indicators

This looks at the measures used by an organisation to assess the performance of its staff. Examples include productivity, absenteeism and labour turnover. The results should be analysed and proposals made for improvements or changes. Candidates should consider:

* **the organisation, and explain it, briefly**

* **the jobs undertaken and the rationale for the performance measures used**

* **the methods used, and explain and analyse these methods**

* **the meaning of the data**

* **the trends shown by the data and draw conclusions**

* **why these trends may have occurred and what improvements might be made.**

A useful starting point is Unit 42 of *Business Studies* by Marcousé *et al.*, Hodder & Stoughton, 1999. Having read it, still be prepared for the fact that different firms measure different personnel indicators. That is fine. Indeed it may become a more interesting project if you are having to explain to the reader about a firm's complex way of measuring staff motivation through, for example, exit interviews.

More than with any other project topic, a vast number of books exist on every aspect of measuring personnel performance. From Taylor and Mayo all the way through to the latest fad for managing human resources. Take care to identify one or two books that assess the theory behind the indicators your firm favours. By comparing your firm's practice to theory, you will be better able to capture the analysis marks on offer.

The other issue with personnel indicators is any difference in perspective between managers and employees. Is there general agreement that the approach taken is fair, effective and comprehensive? Or do staff take a cynical approach to measures they believe to be unreliable and unfair? They may even regard the process more as a symbol of management power rather than an objective attempt to measure performance. Issues such as these can be difficult to handle, especially if your project contact is a personnel manager. In some cases, there may be themes you wish to omit from any report you show the business, leaving such issues to the report you provide to your teacher (and, later, the exam board).

Useful academic starting points for this project include:

*Human Resources and Business Strategy*, Newton A., FT Pitman Books, 1998.

*Managing Best Practice*, No. 56, February 1999, 'Managing the Human Resource Function' published by the Industrial Society (this costs over £100, so request it through your local public library).

*Strategic Human Resourcing*, by Leopold J *et al.*, FT Pitman Books, 1999 (especially Chapter 6 on Performance Management and Chapter 7 on Performance Pay).

## A8  Study of a firm's export performance and prospects

This is a study of a local firm, using its export sales figures broken down by product category and country of destination. The intention is to analyse past performance to form hypotheses about the reasons for successes/failures and to evaluate their implications for future company policy. Candidates should consider:

* **the business, its products, markets and competition**
* **the share of total turnover that exports take (and trends over recent years)**
* **analysing this share further, by product category and destination (trends over time)**
* **hypotheses, for example, sales rising where the local currencies are strong/pound is weak**
* **the reasons behind any identifiable trends following discussions with at least one key executive**
* **implications for future company policy**
* **the conclusions drawn, for example, about the importance of exports for this firm compared with the national average.**

Two issues need to be analysed in relation to the firm's performance and prospects: first, recent trends in the value of sterling, especially in relation to the firm's main export partner countries (it would be worth considering the construction of a specially weighted exchange rate index for the firm); secondly, the potential impact upon the business of British membership of the single european currency, the Euro. Both these issues offer huge scope for research, data presentation and direct analysis. They raise issues that can be assessed through quantitative data and also discussion with key managers. Much of the analysis and the main part of the conclusions to such a project should focus upon the firm's future prospects and policies, not on the past.

Useful academic starting points for this project include:

*The International Business Blueprint*, Monye S., Blackwell, 1997 (especially Chapter 4 on 'International Market Entry Strategies' which includes a list of ten common mistakes made by exporters).

*European Business Handbook*, C.B.I., Kogan Page, 2001 (large reference book containing a series of articles on exporting triumphs, problems and constraints). Too expensive to buy; ask a public library to get hold of it for you.

## TYPE B  THE PROBLEM-SOLVING PROJECT

This requires candidates to identify, quantify, investigate and evaluate how best to solve a problem or make a decision faced by a specific organisation – your contact firm. Examples of this approach include:

**1    Should 'Just For Kids' expand, and if so, how?**

**2    How can 'Debenhams' of Croydon improve its profitability to achieve the standard of other branches in the region?**

**3    How can 'Sports Division' in Northampton improve its stock control?**

Success with projects carried out within an organisation relies a great deal on your ability to coax out sufficient data and staff time. The project on 'Just For Kids', for example, suffered from drawing very little from the small shop it was based on. It used secondary research to look at the market background and a customer questionnaire as the basis for deciding whether or not to expand. The proprietors provided little more than agreement that the survey could take place. Doubtless the project began with assurances of help from the owner, but little help materialised.

By contrast, the Sports Division project was packed with interesting, relevant material about weekly stock levels of Reebok jumpers, Donnay T shirts and much else. It therefore came across as far more businesslike. It gave the sense of a business consultant investigating a problem, rather than a hesitant student peering through the windows of a firm.

A B C D E F G H I J K L M N O P Q R S T U V W X Y Z

## Advantages of Type A1 Feasibility study

☑ forces you to show initiative, which impresses the examiner

☑ you are not reliant on the promises/goodwill of one contact

☑ the method can be followed from the advice given in section WY

## Advantages of Type A2–8 Prescribed project titles

☑ suggested method is set out clearly by the exam board, supplemented by this chapter

☑ business contact will feel clear and confident from the start about the direction of the project

☑ as the method is clear, you will be able to proceed quickly with finding answers

## Advantages of Type B Problem-solving within a firm

☑ a good contact may allow you to use interesting, original data (helping your project to stand out)

☑ comforting and gives you a structure when the project is supported by a contact firm

☑ keeps your costs down, if the firm is covering your photocopying and postage costs

## Disadvantages of Type A1 Feasibility study

☒ daunting to have to initiate so much of what you're doing

☒ there will still be frustrations when people promise data but do not deliver

☒ a study into opening a business as obvious as a newsagent may mean your project fails to stand out

## Disadvantages of Type A2–8 Prescribed project titles

☒ there is a risk that your project may seem rather like others, unless you research it carefully

☒ being provided with the method may make you complacent about how much work there is to do

☒ the suggested method may not fit the issue you are looking at (in which case, change the method)

## Disadvantages of Type B Problem-solving within a firm

☒ despite promises, little data of interest may ever emerge (it is vital to over-come confidentiality early on)

☒ the contact may over- direct your work, making it less interesting for you

☒ your range of research sources may seem very narrow; remember to use primary and secondary sources

# 14.2 Target word length

The rules of the AQA project state clearly: 'approximately 3000 words'. But what does that mean? Are 3500 acceptable? Or even 4000?

At the outset, most students find it hard to think how they will write as many as 3000 words. Towards the end, it is not uncommon for students to find themselves with 7000–12,000 words, with the conclusion, as yet, unwritten!

The reality is that examiners are unlikely to start counting your words. The length will only become an issue if dull, repetitive or unfocused text makes the examiner start yawning, glancing at his/her watch and then thinking about the word count. If you fail to edit your work effectively, the examiner may realise that you have failed to meet the terms of the coursework assessment criteria set out in the syllabus. For example, up to 16 marks are awarded for analysis. To get above eight, your analysis must have been 'selectively using various written and numerate techniques'.

In other words, if your project is over 3000 words because it lacks focus and relevance, the mark scheme will penalise you.

There is one other, less formal reason to stick to the word count. A good project is an interesting project, one that is lively, clear and thoughtful. Long projects become dull to read and hard to follow. Psychologically, you are more likely to get the examiner on your side by being interesting than by being dull.

So how do you make sure you produce a good, analytic project to the right depth, while keeping the word count down. There are five key points to remember:

1   **Set clear objectives from the start.** Most projects wander. The reason being that most students start without clear objectives. So they follow a few trails, analyse the accounts, carry out a customer/staff survey and then wonder what to do with it all. Eventually they decide on their objectives and squeeze their findings in, pretending that they meet the project objectives. This leads to a residue of irrelevant material.

2   **Be ruthless when pruning background information.** You need to start by gaining a full understanding of your business and its marketplace. This does not mean you need to reproduce *all* the data for the examiner. Above all else, make sure that you only include background material that relates directly to your project objectives and method.

3   **Good marks come from showing a skill, not from showing it repeatedly.** You may need to carry out market research to discover some essential information. Done well, this can generate many marks. Yet some students carry out two or even three surveys (or claim they have, anyway). There is virtually no scope for generating extra marks through the repetition of a technique. So plan your project method with care, ensuring that techniques are not repeated.

4   **Edit, rewrite, then re-edit.** In publisher-speak, 'slash and burn!' The psychology of project-writing is clear. You start by writing too much; by padding out sentences and paragraphs to try to meet the apparently huge target of 3000 words. Later you realise you have written 7000 and cannot bear to delete words you have spent so long writing. But you must; your mark depends on it. Reread your background, method and so on. You will find it wordy and boring. Edit, re-write, then re-edit. If someone else will read it for you and point out especially woolly passages, welcome their attention.

5   **Do not skimp on conclusions.** Students tend only to notice the excessive length of their work when they near the end of the report. By this time there is little more to do than smarten it up and write a conclusion. Now, no one likes writing conclusions so there is a strong temptation to say, 'Well, I've already written 5000 words, so I'll just do a brief conclusion'. Yet the AQA coursework marking criteria allocate 40% of the total mark to synthesis and evaluation – both skills which are tightly bound up in your recommendations and conclusions. It is crazy, therefore, to skimp on conclusions; prune the early part of the report, not the key later parts.

## 14.3 The AQA assessment criteria

It is always important to know how a piece of work is to be marked. Is accurate knowledge the key criterion for success? Or is it evaluation? Although the same question arises for the AQA coursework, there is one proviso. It is the overriding instruction to teachers and examiners that 'each project should be marked as a whole rather than as a sum of isolated parts'. So although it is valuable to read each of the marking criteria with care, the key to success is for the project to have coherence. It should never end up being a patchwork of points made to meet the exam board criteria.

The overall marking structure for the AQA project is:

|  | Marks (out of 84) | Percentage marks |
|---|---|---|
| Knowledge and understanding | 16 | 19% |
| Application of knowledge/methodology | 16 | 19% |
| Analysis of evidence | 16 | 19% |
| Synthesis | 10 | 12% |
| Evaluation | 22 | 26% |
| Quality of language | 4 | 5% |

## KNOWLEDGE AND UNDERSTANDING (16 MARKS)

To score 13–16 marks, you need to 'include relevant material, focused clearly on the project objective, fully explained and presented appropriately'. This is demanding, but not impossible. The easy part should be showing your understanding by explaining the material fully. Do not just include your contact firm's latest accounts; explain what they mean and what they show. Remember, though, that you do not need to explain everything fully, otherwise the 3000 words will soon be used up. The same applies to 'presented appropriately'. Turning sales figures into graphs can be valuable, but there is no need to turn every table of figures into a chart.

The key issue, then, is relevance. In other words 'relevant material, focused clearly on the project objective'. Lots of background knowledge will not be enough to get you the top mark. You must select the aspects which are relevant to fulfilling the project objectives. Two pages of well selected material are worth more than six pages of unedited work.

For instance, the background to a project on opening a golf driving range included full details (and many diagrams) of:

1    **the number of golfers in the UK (and trends over the past three years)**

2    **trends in the number of driving ranges in Europe and America**

3    **the number of golf courses in the UK**

4    **trends in the amount spent on golf equipment each year**

5    **the opening hours and prices charged at four local driving ranges**

6    **a demographic profile of golfers.**

This material occupied five pages and 1100 words. After much heartache, the student agreed to cut out 3, 4, and 6. The result was a far better focused, more impressive background of 600 words. The project received full marks for knowledge and understanding.

# APPLICATION OF KNOWLEDGE/METHODOLOGY (16 MARKS)

To achieve top marks on this criterion, you must show:

'Clear evidence of relevant, valid research drawn from primary and secondary sources – showing a strong grasp of theory and the ability to comment critically on the methods used' (13–16 marks).

This is a very demanding statement. It requires the following:

- **'clear evidence of relevant, valid research ...', in other words the research must be related directly to meeting your project objectives and the research method must be logical and academically sound. Also the evidence of both these qualities must be clear; a key issue is whether you genuinely carried out the fieldwork you are reporting on. It will be no news to you that some students invent their research 'findings', so you should provide evidence such as filled-in questionnaires (in an appendix) or a highly detailed explanation of your research process. Show you really did carry out the research.**

- **'... drawn from primary and secondary sources' is self-explanatory; note that this research must still be relevant. Throwing in some secondary data will be no use unless you make it clear how it relates to your project objectives.**

- **'... showing strong grasp of theory ...', implies giving a full justification of the choices you make on theoretical grounds. For example, why *exactly* did you choose a quota sample rather than random? Why use NPV rather than ARR? Citing text books in support of your decisions is likely to strengthen your academic case.**

- **'... comment critically on the methods used' is easy to do, but hard to do well. The secret is – as above – to find an academic source for your criticisms; if your primary research sample was small, you could point it out as a weakness. Far better, though, to quote a source such as the *A–Z Business Studies Handbook* which says: 'Sample size is important as it needs to be large enough to make the data statistically valid. A sample of 20 people, for example, is so small that a different 20 people could easily have quite separate views'.**

# ANALYSIS OF EVIDENCE (16 MARKS)

Analysis means breaking something down into its component parts, to help identify and understand causes, effects and implications. The maximum marks for analysis come from:

'Substantial analysis of the data, selectively using various written and numerate techniques to identify causes and/or possible solutions and showing judgement in the techniques used' (13–16 marks).

The above statement contains what may appear a contradiction. The analysis must be 'substantial' yet applied 'selectively'. The difference is between quantity and quality. Top marks come from the ability to choose and justify the right way of analysing each problem – as compared to a shotgun approach, in which every possible technique is used.

If analysing market research findings, consider breaking them down into sub-groups (i.e. look at the figures not only in total, but perhaps broken down into men and women). Do not, however, break every question down into every possible sub-group.

If considering an investment decision, do not feel that you have to use investment appraisal, break-even and projected financial accounts. Much of this would be pointless duplication.

The correct approach is to think hard about your own business, its financial and other circumstances and choose the appropriate technique. If cash flow is a problem, for example, you should use pay-back as a means of investment appraisal. If a new product launch or a feasibility study rests upon market research as the only method of sales forecasting, analysing the statistical reliability of the findings is of paramount importance.

Beware of confusing 'substantial analysis' with 'death by numbers/graphs'. Examiners hate number overkill as much as most students.

# SYNTHESIS (10 MARKS)

These marks are important because they are accessible to everyone. Even if your research has not worked out well or your contact has let you down, you can still fully meet this criterion: 'The project's structure is well thought through, making it easy to follow the logic, the communication and the recommendations which draw together the most appropriate evidence and arguments.' (8–10 marks).

Few projects live up to this, largely because students tackle their coursework so late that the week before the deadline is a mad panic to finish off the findings, recommendations and graphs. It would be so much better if that time were spent improving communication aspects of the report, using techniques such as:

- **summary tables showing how your method fits in with your objectives, for example:**

| Objectives | Corresponding methods |
|---|---|
| Objective 1 – To identify and cost the start-up expenses on the proposed nightclub … | Method 1. Make appointments with two nightclub owners, an estate agent and a builder. |
| Objective 2 – To forecast sales revenue for the nightclub's first four years … | Method 2. Survey 16–21-year-olds locally; use 90/30 rule* to forecast demand; use survey and knowledge from rival nightclub owners to set price; use *Mintel*s forecast of market trends to work out revenue in years 2–4. |

*See Business Calculations and Statistics, Marcousé, I., Longman 1994

- **cross-referencing within your report, helping to lead the reader through the work**

- **not too much use of company jargon, avoiding excessive use of acronyms (initials such as ARR). Where such terms are needed, make sure to use a running glossary; this means building up a glossary at the foot of the pages, so the reader does not lose track**

- **a contents page, page numbers and possibly even section dividers – all give the reader confidence that the structure is carefully thought through**

- **constructive use of appendices, ensuring that lengthy or repetitive calculations are put there, yet referred to within the text**

- **summaries of key findings and conclusions as you go through each section of your report; this is very helpful to the reader, who may be struggling through his/her fourth project that night**

- **a section entitled 'recommendations'; an evaluation/conclusion section should be in addition to this.**

# EVALUATION (22 MARKS)

Evaluation means judgement. In other words your ability to weigh up evidence, place different factors in order of importance and reach final conclusions. Evaluation skills can also be assessed from the judgement you show in your use of words, concepts and forms of presentation.

The marking criteria contains the following sentence to explain how to achieve the highest mark for evaluation:

> 'appropriate conclusions justified by the evidence, showing an awareness of the most relevant underlying themes or issues and their potential implications for the business concerned' (18–22 marks).

This difficult criterion is to ensure that exceptional projects can be distinguished from very good ones. Few candidates are likely to match this wording, yet its meaning is quite easy to explain:

* **'appropriate conclusions justified by the evidence.' This means that the conclusions must be rooted in the findings of the project, i.e. your analysis. Many conclusions follow similar, teacher-directed lines such as 'What I learned from doing this project was ...'. For the top mark, the key is to develop a conclusion based upon the problem you have tackled, not on a formula.**

* **'potential implications for the business concerned.' This suggests looking carefully at the longer term, underlying consequences of the recommendations you have made or the conclusions you have drawn. For instance, a project on labour turnover may have led to the conclusion that the management culture was too Taylorite; you may go a step further and point out that for as long as senior management adopt such an approach, middle and junior managers will follow. Therefore until there are personnel changes at the top it may be unrealistic to expect change lower down.**

Achieving these criteria is demanding, but should be possible, as long as you give yourself enough time to draft and re-draft a full, thoughtful conclusion, preferably after discussion with others.

# QUALITY OF LANGUAGE (4 MARKS)

The ability to draft and re-draft, plus the use of spell and grammar checks, should make these marks easy to acquire. The top achievement level of 4 out of 4 requires that:

'Complex ideas are expressed clearly and fluently. Sentences and paragraphs follow on from one another smoothly and logically. Arguments are consistently relevant and well structured. There are few, if any, errors of grammar, punctuation and spelling.'

## 14.4 Internally assessed but externally moderated

Your teachers have to mark all the projects from your school/college. If there is more than one class studying AQA Business Studies, staff must agree on a single list of marks across all the classes. For this to occur, each teacher has not only to read and mark all the projects from their own class, but those from other classes too. This is a very time-consuming (and stressful) process. Therefore it is important that you should make sure to complete your report by the deadline set by staff.

Internal assessment has other implications for you. Teachers are inevitably influenced by the effort you have put in. They look to reward those who have researched thoroughly and honestly, and those who have worked hard on editing, re-writing and on presentation. If projects are marked externally, there is a greater chance that last-minute, largely invented work will slip past the unsuspecting examiner. Internal assessment gives you no hiding place. This leads to an inevitable conclusion: work hard, work early, involve your teacher, accept the advice given and make sure you meet deadlines. Good Projects come from healthy cooperation between student and teacher/mentor.

## SUMMARY: HOW TO MAKE THE MOST OF THE AQA PROJECT
### 1 What makes a great project?

There are three main features:

a   A project should have clear objectives, a valid method, findings which are analysed relevantly and conclusions that are thought-provoking, yet stem logically from the rest of the work.

b   The report should be clearly expressed, easy to follow (and cross-reference) and pursue a straight path from the objective through to the findings.

c   The report should be edited ruthlessly. Wordy sentences should be pruned; irrelevant material cut completely; graphs and diagrams limited to those that add to analysis or understanding.

## 2 How should project objectives be expressed?

A good approach is to state your primary objective (which must be closely related to the project title), then set out (and explain) the secondary objectives required to achieve the primary one.

For example:

**Project title: Should ZBC Co. buy the vacant property next door?**

**Primary objective:**

To make fully justified recommendations to the directors of ZBC Co. as to whether they should buy the vacant property next door.

**Secondary objectives:**

a   Examine ZBC Co.'s accounts to see whether the purchase can be afforded.

b   Identify the alternative uses ZBC Co. could make of the site.

c   Shortlist the uses that fit in with the firm's plans.

d   Forecast the revenues and costs that could be generated by the shortlisted uses.

e   Analyse and evaluate the figures in objective c in terms of profit, breakeven and cash flow.

f   Conduct an investment appraisal, comparing the best use of the site with the cost of buying it.

## 3 Are students penalised if the project is too long?

Yes, possibly. If you have selected a suitable project and written concisely, it should be possible to present a report of around 3000 words. Over-long projects tend to penalise themselves because they lack focus. Writing everything you know about the ZBC Co. would generate as poor a coursework mark as it would an essay mark. You show good analysis by choosing and using the right technique in the right way – not by using lots of techniques, some of which are inappropriate.

So, if you have already written over 6000 words, now is the time to prune out the marginal points and prune back those 25-word sentences to 15 words. All good writing comes from cutting and then cutting again.

## 4 How should market research findings be presented?

**a** Don't put the results together in a whole section, with table after table of findings. This bores the reader and cannot move you up the levels of response ladder to a good grade.

**b** Use your research findings where they are relevant to a particular part of the project. If your Q6 asks about likelihood of purchasing, use the results in the section on sales forecasting.

**c** Don't feel you have to justify then analyse the results to every question. Often a question yields no useful finding. Say so, and get on to something more fruitful.

**d** Be imaginative about graphs. Think of ways to help the reader understand the significance of findings. In particular, important findings deserve important looking graphs. Most graphs, however, are better kept small, as an insert within your text, rather than on a full page.

## 5 How should the project be written up?

The writing style should be like a business report. In other words the text should be organised into sections and subsections, with a clear numbering system to help the reader follow your thought processes. You, the writer, should then make use of that system. For example, by explaining how a part of your findings helps achieve 'sub-objective 2.3' or whatever.

A common mistake with reports is to make the paragraphs too brief. High marks for analysis and evaluation are likely to require well-developed arguments. So beware of making your report entirely in point form.

## 6 Useful extras

Projects are enhanced by a few, quite simple extras:

**a** **Bibliography:** a list of any books, magazines, in-house (business) reports or documents that have provided information used in your work. Ideally, you will have made direct reference to these in the relevant part of your project.

**b** **Glossary:** there is no need to explain the meaning of terms listed in business dictionaries or A–Zs, but there may be other jargon terms requiring explanation. For example, one large UK company uses the term 'associates' for fellow members of staff. If your report refers to an unusual usage or term such as this, provide a glossary to help the reader.

c    **Appendices:** above all, use these sparingly; quantity/bulk does not turn examiners on, it puts them off. Only include in an appendix material which you have referred to in the main text. For example, you might include in your project introduction a graph showing the sales trend for the company over the past three years. The appendix could contain the raw, monthly data.

d    **Contents and paging:** every project should have a contents page and numbered pages.

# 7  How long should the conclusions be?

A surprising number of projects have very brief conclusions. Some consist of little more than a feeble attempt to suck up to the examiner ('I enjoyed doing this project very much because …').

Please take the issue of conclusions very seriously. They are very important to your marks and grades throughout this AS/A level course. The typical project contains less than a side of conclusions, yet surely your experience has been rich enough to provide a great deal of thoughtful reflection.

Among the possible lines of thought are:

* **What have I learnt about the company?**

* **What have I learnt about business theory in practice?**

* **What have I learnt about the process of completing a project?**

* **What should the firm do next? What is it likely to do next? Why the mismatch (if any)?**

* **How well did I meet my objectives (and why)?**

* **What extra could/should I have done if the resources existed (time and money, for example)?**

## 14.5  Conclusions

A good project is an interesting read; interesting because the reader learns something from it, either about a specific firm or about an interesting new way to apply business theory. A report full of descriptive company history or an overload of figures can never fit the bill.

Mentioned at the start was the need for a focused, 'straight line' approach from objectives through to recommendations and conclusions. Keep bearing that in mind as you edit your material down to the required length. Does that ratio analysis do anything? Do those interviews lead anywhere? And so on.

Ultimately the project is no more than an answer to the question posed by its title. So make sure it is answered fully, with clear evidence to support your arguments. In that respect a project report is not so different from an essay.

A
B
C
D
E
F
G
H
I
J
K
L
M
N
O
P
Q
R
S
T
U
V
W
X
Y
Z

# The OCR (Cambridge) business project

This section sets out what you need to know to get a high grade on the Cambridge project. It is written on the assumption that you have already read Chapters 1–13 of this book.

The OCR project has several distinctive features, each of which will be explained fully:

**1**  **a clear statement of required project contents**

**2**  **a traditional emphasis on problem solving, which often entails numerical analysis**

**3**  **a target word length of 'about 4000 words'**

**4**  **fully explained marking criteria, which place heavy emphasis on business concepts and methodology**

**5**  **submission of proposed titles to the exam board**

**6**  **teacher-marked, but moderated externally by the exam board.**

## 15.1  Clear statement of required project contents

The syllabus gives the following advice:

'The report must:

* **be investigative in nature, showing problem-solving skills**

* **be based either on a single organisation or on a more general business-related issue**

* **use, analytically and with evaluation, business studies knowledge drawn from various elements of the course as appropriate to the selected problem**

* **be presented as a report with clear definition of the problem and objectives in pursuing it.'**

The project should be written up as a report and should have a clear decision-making framework within which there can easily be found:

- a title which accurately reflects the work undertaken

- a setting for the problem

- a clear definition of the problem

- the candidate's objectives in relation to the problem

- relevant information collected in a suitable manner

- the development, and where necessary substantiation, of relevant and appropriate criteria for evaluation

- the use of theory as required, e.g. to support criteria, to argue the use of given techniques and to evaluate the information

- the use of appropriate methods of evaluation

- analysis, evaluation or synthesis in the light of the objectives set and the information gathered

- the development of conclusions which are valid in the light of the evidence which is submitted and the arguments presented

- a recommendation

- a general framework of communication which makes it easy for the reader to absorb the main features of the report and to refer backwards and forwards as necessary.

The reality is less daunting than this list. Most high-grade assignments are written from a far less academic standpoint. Nevertheless, the above list represents the best way to achieve success in an OCR project. Table 15.1 below provides a commentary on each of the points made.

**Table 15.1** The elements within the Cambridge decision making project framework

| Project element | Explanation and elaboration |
| --- | --- |
| Title | a working title should be decided early on in the project process; the final title may change later to reflect the actual analysis you achieved |
| Setting | explaining the background to the business problem or opportunity – probably based on company data and secondary research |

| | |
|---|---|
| Defining the problem | explaining the business situation surrounding the problem or opportunity (the causes, the effects and their magnitude) |
| Objectives | the primary and secondary objectives set to tackle the project (see Chapter 5 for full details) |
| Relevant information | explaining the method and process of data collection to achieve the objectives, setting out clearly how the research was undertaken |
| Decision-making criteria | setting and justifying a hypothesis which can be used as the yardstick for decision making |
| Business theory | setting out the theoretical issues underpinning your research method, your decision making criteria and your means of evaluating the project recommendations |
| Techniques of evaluation | making effective use of decision-making methods such as investment appraisal or breakeven analysis |
| Analysis and evaluation | reflecting critically upon the decision-making method and its results in the light of the project objectives |
| Conclusions | reaching conclusions which flow logically from your preceding arguments and address all the objectives you set |
| Recommendation | advising the firm on what actions to take (note that these do not have to be firm; you may argue that more research is needed before proceeding) |
| Communication framework | this affects the assignment from the first page to the last; good communication and presentation for projects is tackled in Chapter 13 |

It is important to note that the Cambridge Board uses the term 'problem' in the way it is used in maths rather than in business. 'Solving a problem' means 'finding an answer to the question'. It is perfectly valid, therefore, to produce an assignment about a business opportunity. The starting point does not have to be a 'problem business'. For example, the Board's list of suggested titles includes the following:

- Should a local filling station convert to 24-hour service?
- Is there scope for a new vegetarian restaurant in ...?
- Should Middlewell Fertilisers introduce flexible working?

## 15.2 Emphasis on problem solving and therefore numerical analysis

The OCR project is a decision making exercise. Your task is to identify a decision which needs to be made, then devise a method for making it. If the decision is substantial enough, real businesses would use numerical (probably financial) criteria if at all possible. Therefore it is expected that you will do the same. This has some important benefits. The marking criteria are based on your ability to analyse and evaluate a problem that can be judged against a yardstick you have set. Therefore you should follow a model such as:

1 set a yardstick, for example, reducing labour turnover to 12%

2 conduct research, for example, break labour turnover data down by department and carry out a staff questionnaire on motivation

3 identify and cost recommendations for cutting the turnover in the worst departments

4 make fully costed recommendations on how to reduce labour turnover to 12%.

This model is rooted in quantification of the problem and the solution, exactly as a professional manager would tackle it. It also fits perfectly not only the marking criteria, but also the examiners' expectations. A project with little or no quantification could in theory achieve a high mark, but will rarely do so in practice.

This points to certain conclusions:

1 Ensure from the start that your contact company is prepared to allow you access to its financial or other quantified data; alternatively, will it allow you to gather your own, e.g. through a survey of its staff or customers?

2 Look for a project title that can be answered in a quantified way. How, for example, could you quantify: 'How should the communication methods and patterns in XXX Ltd be changed to cope with recent growth?' This is an interesting business question, but it will lead to

written assessment rather than quantified analysis. Beware of such titles.

3  Discuss with your teacher an appropriate method of numerical analysis, then read up on it so that you develop a very good understanding of the theory involved. Remember that teachers work within tight time constraints; there may be many more useful aspects to a theory than have been taught in class.

4  Always be willing to change your project title if the figures you expected are withheld by your contact company.

## 15.3  A target word length of 'about 4000'

At the outset, most students find it hard to think how they will write as many as 4000 words. Towards the end, it is not uncommon for students to find themselves with 7000–12000 words, with the conclusion, as yet, unwritten.

Of course, examiners are unlikely to start counting your words. So does it matter if you overrun? The length will only become an issue if dull, repetitive or unfocused text makes the examiner start yawning, glancing at the watch and then thinking about the word count. If you have failed to edit your work effectively, the examiner may realise that you have failed to meet the terms of the 'coursework assessment criteria' set out in the syllabus. For example, up to fifteen marks are awarded for 'selectivity, analysis and synthesis'. So, if your project is over 4000 words because it lacks focus and relevance, the mark scheme will penalise you.

There is one other, less formal reason to stick to the word count. A good project is an interesting project. One that is lively, clear and thoughtful. Long projects become dull to read and hard to follow. Psychologically, you are more likely to get the examiner on your side by being interesting than by being dull.

So how do you make sure you produce a good, analytic project with the right depth, while keeping the word count down. There are five key points to remember:

1  **Set clear objectives from the start. Most projects wander because students start without clear objectives. So they follow a few trails, analyse the accounts, carry out a customer/staff survey and then wonder what to do with it all. Eventually they decide on their objectives, and squeeze their findings in, pretending that they meet the project objectives. This ensures an excess of irrelevant material.**

2   **Be ruthless at pruning background information.** You need to start by gaining a full understanding of your business and its marketplace. That does not mean you need to reproduce all this data for the examiner. Above all else, make sure that you only include background material which relates directly to your project objectives and method.

3   **Good marks come from showing a skill, not from showing it repeatedly.** You may need to carry out market research to discover some essential information. Done well, this can generate many marks. Yet some students carry out two or even three surveys (or claim they have, anyway). There is virtually no scope for generating extra marks through the repetition of a technique. So plan your project method with care, ensuring that techniques are not repeated.

4   **Edit, rewrite, then re-edit.** In publisher-speak: 'slash and burn!' The psychology of project-writing is clear. You start by writing too much, by padding out sentences and paragraphs attempting to meet this apparently huge target of 4000 words. Later you realise you have written 7000 and cannot bear to delete words you have spent so long writing. But you must; your mark depends on it. Reread your background, method and so on. You will find it wordy and boring. Edit, re-write, then re-edit. If someone else will read it for you and point out especially woolly passages, welcome their attentions.

5   **Do not skimp on conclusions.** Students tend only to notice the excessive length of their work when they near the end of the report, by which time there is little more to do than smarten it up and write a conclusion. Now, no one likes writing conclusions, so there is a great temptation to say: 'Well, I've already written 5000 words, so I'll just do a brief conclusion.' Yet the OCR coursework assessment criteria allocate over 20% of the total mark to synthesis and evaluation – both skills which are tightly bound up in your recommendations and conclusions. It is crazy, therefore, to skimp on conclusions. Prune the early part of the report, not the key later parts.

## 15.4 Marking criteria, which place heavy emphasis on business concepts and methodology

Shown below are the OCR syllabus marking criteria used for the research assignment, shown below. Notice the importance of identifying and applying relevant business concepts (points 3, 4 and 5). Together, these represent 35/90; that is more than 40% of all the marks available.

| Marking criterion | Maximum marks |
|---|---|
| 1 The skill with which the problem has been explained in context (background) | 5 |
| 2 The skill with which appropriate and realistic objectives have been set and used | 10 |
| 3 Evidence of appropriate research methods | 10 |
| 4 Evidence of appropriate primary and secondary research | 10 |
| 5 Evidence of understanding and use of appropriate business studies knowledge | 15 |
| 6 Selectivity, analysis and synthesis | 15 |
| 7 Evaluation, recommendation or strategy development | 15 |
| 8 Presentation | 5 |
| 9 Written communication skills | 5 |
| Total | 90 |

1 **Background.** This is covered fully in Chapter 7.

2 **The skill with which appropriate and realistic objectives have been set and used.** This is covered fully in Chapter 5. OCR adds that candidates should 'set objectives for the investigation as a whole and for the distinct stages of it'. This fits in with the emphasis in Chapter 5 on splitting primary objectives (the investigation as a whole) from secondary objectives (the distinct stages of the project). A further point made by OCR is that 'the success of the investigation should also be assessed by comparing actual achievements with the intended outcomes'.

3 **Evidence of appropriate research methods.** The Cambridge approach is for students to get directly involved in a business. This suggests you look around, question people, look at relevant statistical data, then work from within the business at solving the problem set. The secret to effective research is that it should be relevant to the objectives. The mark scheme shows that top marks require that 'a method of approach has been selected and effectively justified in the context of the problem and its potential solutions'. Chapter 6 explains how to do exactly that.

4   **Evidence of appropriate primary and secondary research.** Note the wording in this heading. As the OCR syllabus spells out, 'Sufficient primary research will be expected but it should be supplemented by appropriate secondary research including specialist reading around the topic'. It is also recommended that candidates 'make good use of the Internet as a source' of data; the websites on pages 190–193 may help here. Secondary and primary research are explained in detail in Chapters 8 and 9.

5   **Evidence of understanding and use of appropriate business studies knowledge.** In other words, when tackling your project, are you using correctly the language and concepts of the subject? Some projects are well written and sensible, but only as a student of English might make sense of a week or two spent at a business. English students could describe, even analyse, what they have seen and heard. But there would be little evidence of business theory. So these 15 marks are there to encourage you to 'show off' your classroom and text book knowledge.

One would expect the typical project to be full of terms such as:

*strategy, authority, capacity, opportunity cost, hierarchy, niche, plan, capital, resources, criterion level, customer service, focus,* and so on. For definitions of these, see *The Complete A–Z Business Studies Handbook* 3rd Edition, Hodder & Stoughton, 2000.

6   **Selectivity, analysis and synthesis.** OCR states that 'this criterion assesses the candidate's ability to turn data into evidence, to reject some which will not be relevant, to draw some together (synthesis) and to break other bits down and interpret them (analysis)'. In other words, these marks are for how well you use data (sophisticated analysis, as set out in Chapter 11), how well you judge its value, and how well you bring it together, to help the reader to see the whole picture.

7   **Evaluation, recommendation or strategy development.** This aspect of the project is covered fully in Chapter 12. To gain the top level on this criterion, OCR requires that 'reasoning and logic are of a high standard throughout the work'. Vital though this is, most of the marks will stem from the conclusion itself. With OCR projects it is important to ensure that the recommendations and conclusions you draw are strictly relevant to the project objectives. This can be done through a summary table which matches conclusions to the original project goals.

8    **Presentation.** Although this seems quite a low mark allocation (just 5 marks), don't be fooled. If the reader struggles to follow your train of thought because the work is hard to follow, there is little chance of good analysis or evaluation marks. It is important that the reader should find the assignment interesting. If the report is interesting he or she will start looking for the strengths, not the flaws. So do make the effort to present your work well. OCR asks for 'an accurate title at the front, work sectioned into paragraphs, diagrams labelled and explained, statistics and other data sourced and quotations attributed'. See Chapter 13 for further guidance.

9    **Written communication skills.** This is assessed in relation to three qualities:

   ● the clarity of the candidate's expression

   ● the structure and presentation of ideas

   ● accuracy of grammar, punctuation and spelling

To score five out of five, the report must be consistently well written and structured, given that the candidate can check the work at leisure. By implication, spelling mistakes and confusing sentences will be penalised quite severely. This is another reason why it is important to complete the bulk of your work comfortably before the final deadline looms. Spelling mistakes, typos and woolly logic will cost marks.

## 15.5  Written submission of proposed titles

OCR invites teachers to submit their students' proposed assignment titles for comment by a senior examiner. This process is especially valuable if the teacher or, even more, the school/college, is new to business studies. Experienced teachers can feel confident in their ability to judge what will make a good project.

It is recommended that proposed titles are submitted six months before the assignment completion date. Given that the Board says it will take up to six weeks to supply its comments, an earlier submission is obviously worthwhile.

OCR has learned over the years that some students feel bound by the project title once it has been approved by the Board. Please do not. Changing circumstances may require a change in title. Your teacher can help advise you on this.

## 15.6 Internally assessed but externally moderated

Your teacher(s) have to mark all the projects from your school/college. If there is more than one class studying business studies, staff must agree on a single list of marks across all the classes. For this to occur, each teacher has not only to read and mark all the projects from their own class, but also from others. Therefore it is important that you should make sure to complete your report by the deadline set by staff.

Internal assessment has other implications for you. Teachers are inevitably influenced by the effort you have put in. They look to reward those who have researched thoroughly and honestly, and those who have worked hard on editing, re-writing and on presentation. If projects are marked externally, there is a greater chance that last-minute, largely invented work will slip past the unsuspecting examiner. Internal assessment gives you no hiding place. This leads to an inevitable conclusion: work hard, work early, involve your teacher, accept the advice given and make sure to meet deadlines. Good projects come from healthy cooperation between student and teacher/mentor.

## 15.7 Conclusion

When marking the OCR Project teachers and external moderators are advised to view the project as a whole. In other words to judge whether it is a good piece of work (rather than just a collection of good parts). For your report to be impressive as a whole, it will need to be written clearly, to use the language and concepts of business but, above all else, to be focused clearly upon the project objectives. So be willing to press the delete button on irrelevant material.

# The Edexcel coursework option

This section sets out what you need to know to get a high grade on the Edexcel project. It is written on the assumption that you have already read Chapters 1–13 of this book.

Edexcel coursework has several distinctive features, each of which will be explained fully:

1  **a choice of one out of two set titles; these titles will change from year to year**

2  **a target word length of approximately 3000 and no more than 3500 words**

3  **fully explained marking criteria, which place heavy emphasis on analysis and evaluation**

4  **assessment by the candidate's teacher, but moderated (checked) by the exam board.**

The Edexcel Notes For Guidance point out that a successful coursework assignment should:

● **'show evidence of individual enquiry, analysis and evaluation ...'**

● **demonstrate an integration of both primary and secondary research with appropriate techniques and concepts drawn from relevant parts of the syllabus ...**

● **make recommendations for action that the firm could adopt, where these are appropriate'.**

The exam board goes on to emphasise the need for valid research, with the method and sources explained and a careful assessment of the validity and reliability of the findings. A key sentence states that: 'candidates should be reminded of the importance of explaining their course of action when undertaking research'.

## 16.1 Your choice between the different types of Edexcel project

### COURSEWORK ONE: BUSINESS PLANNING

Each year Edexcel specifies three possible business opportunities. In the Edexcel teachers' and coursework guide the three suggested are a café, a hairdressing salon and a video shop. Candidates choose one of these, then carry out a feasibility study into whether the new business opportunity is financially viable. This requires independent primary and secondary research, which helps to generate the evidence required for high marks. Sample titles might include:

- **An investigation into the financial viability of opening a new cyber-café.**

- **A business plan for opening a hairdressing salon at John Leggott College**

- **Now the local Blockbuster outlet has closed down, is it viable to open a new, independent video shop?**

Feasibility studies are explained fully in Chapter 17. Each year Edexcel spells out exactly how the business plan/feasibility study should be tackled. A read through Chapter 17 will establish several keys to all effective plans for business start-ups:

- **gaining a good enough understanding of local competition and local consumers to position your business effectively (a 'situational audit'); it is no good just starting 'a café' – if it is not focused upon a specific type of customer it is very unlikely to succeed; therefore a clear marketing strategy is vital**

- **forecasting cash flows to identify how much finance will be required to survive the difficult early phases in the life of every business**

- **a businesslike method for assessing whether the business is financially viable in the medium–long term; this is usually done through break-even analysis or investment appraisal.**

### COURSEWORK TWO: A SPECIFIED TASK AT A LOCAL BUSINESS

The Edexcel coursework guide gives the example of a project at a local manufacturing firm. You are required to gain sufficient understanding of the business to write a report on how it would respond to a new situation. The sample version suggests that you: 'assume this firm wishes to expand its product portfolio and this decision would involve an increase in the number of people it employs at all levels. Present a report for the board of directors detailing the main elements of human resource planning which will be involved in the following areas: a new production manager; new marketing personnel; production workers. Your report should include job specifications and descriptions, selection methods, induction and training – all in the context of your local labour market'.

In an exercise such as this, the absolute key to high marks will be your ability to get the most from what may only be one or two visits to the business in question. Read Chapters 3 and 4 with care, but also bear in mind the following:

- **Make sure you question your guides/speakers in enough detail to understand exactly what the firm does, what its key strengths and weaknesses are, how it operates internally (management style, organisational structure, methods of remuneration, methods of production, quality control and stock control) and where it sees its future.**

- **Your project can only impress if you show some depth of understanding of the way the firm is managed.**

- **To obtain a top grade, your research and write-up must be able to generate the ambitious statements set out in the Edexcel assessment criteria (mark scheme), set out as follows in 16.2.**

## 16.2 Assessment criteria

Edexcel coursework is marked under four headings. Each is set out below, as is the description given of how to achieve the top marks.

### 1 Demonstrate knowledge and critical understanding of the specified content

Mark range 17–20 out of 20 if the candidate 'shows detailed evidence of information used from <u>available sources</u> together with effective use of such information to demonstrate <u>critical understanding</u> of the specified content'.

The two key statements are underlined. Top marks are only available to students who have gathered material from available sources (note the plural). This is easy to achieve when carrying out a business plan into the feasibility of starting up a new business, as the research has to be wide and varied. It may be harder when visiting a firm. Be careful of depending too much on one speaker's views.

The same issue arises with the second phrase underlined. Critical understanding is almost impossible if you have only one viewpoint to base your research upon. Ideally you want a variety of views from a variety of people within the business, from chief executive to trainee. If the boss is proud of the induction programme, but the trainee seems ill-informed and poorly motivated, that provides scope for you to show your critical understanding of the situation.

**Key point**: make sure to obtain a range of views from a range of people.

**2  Apply knowledge and understanding to problems and issues arising from both familiar and unfamiliar situations**

Mark range 17–20 out of 20 if the candidate 'shows the application of detailed knowledge and critical understanding to issues arising from the problem, underpinned by synthesis of theory'.

Again, the two key statements are underlined. Application is the test of whether you can relate your knowledge to the business context and to the objectives of your project. In this case the exam board wants to see theory applied to the problem, for example using critical path analysis to plan the opening of the café, or a decision tree to help choose between alternative approaches to solving a problem. For further examples, read the first two pages of Chapter 10.

**Key point**: plan how to apply theory to the project, then gather the data needed to carry out the analysis.

**3  Analyse problems, issues and situations**

Mark range 17–20 out of 20 if the candidate 'analyses problems, issues arising and situations, making valid suggestions as to the data required for a full analysis'.

The first of the underlined phrases states the obvious, but is still worth careful consideration. Chapters 10 and 11 of this book look at how to analyse successfully. The skill of analysis can be shown by constructing a complex argument, especially if it reveals the real causes or effects of a problem. For project work, however, it is often easier to achieve high marks for analysis by using a business method that is considered analytic by examiners. A good example is investment appraisal. Logically gathered cash flow data analysed through pay-back period, ARR or NPV will assure the examiner of your analytic skills.

The second underlined section is interesting, as it shows acceptance of the practical limits of any student project. You cannot be expected to survey hundreds of people or visit customers' warehouses throughout Britain. To achieve top level marks you should think through with care the research that the company would need to carry out before risking their capital on whatever recommendations you are inclined towards. This should include the sample sizes you recommend and the manpower you believe would be needed. For instance, 'to complete this appraisal effectively, it is likely to require several weeks' work by an executive senior enough to talk to the decision makers at the client companies and to gain access to all the financial data'.

Although not stated at the top mark level, it is worth noting that the second level marks (11–15 out of 20) require an appreciation of 'the limitations of the data'. It is very likely that examiners will want the same understanding shown at the top level. So do be critical of your own data – especially if it has been gathered through your own market research survey. A careful read of Chapter 9 will help here.

**Key point:** gather data to enable you to undertake analysis using business methods and be willing to point out how the firm should complete the task before putting its capital at risk.

### 4 Evaluate, distinguish between fact and opinion, and assess information from a variety of sources

Top level marks of 16–20 out of 20 require that the candidate 'evaluates and distinguishes between fact and opinion and offers a valid recommendation based on the synthesis of the available information'.

This statement is packed with key points. To take each in turn:

- **Here 'evaluates' means makes judgements, either on the evidence presented or on the wider aspects of what you have learned. For instance, what started off as a project on stock control may end up with you realising that the underlying cause of poor stock management was lack of staff motivation.**

- **The phrase 'distinguishes between fact and opinion' indicates a skill that should come through in every part of your project report. When gathering data, be sure to put in quotation marks anything that was actually said by a manager, remembering to consider whether the statement was based on fact or opinion. Managers** are prone to say things such as 'we operate on democratic principles'. Even if the manager believes what he/she is saying, it may not be a fact. If you can consistently distinguish between fact and opinion, this will help your marks enormously.

- The words 'offers a valid recommendation' highlight the need to both make a recommendation (see Section 12.3) and ensure its validity in the context of the problem, the situation of the business and the analysis you have already completed.

- By 'synthesis of all the available information' it is meant that the recommendations you make should be based upon the summary you have made of your own findings. Therefore a conclusion should start with a section headed 'Synthesis of Findings' before going on to make recommendations based upon that synthesis.

**Key point:** the demands of the mark scheme mean that your conclusions and recommendations should be substantial, perhaps 500–750 words.

## 16.3 Target word length

The rules of the Edexcel project are clear, 'about 3000 words but no more than 3500'.

At the outset, most students find it hard to think how they will write as many as 3000 words. Towards the end, it is not uncommon for students to find themselves with 7000–12,000 words, with the conclusion, as yet, unwritten!

The reality is that examiners are unlikely to start counting your words. The length will only become an issue if dull, repetitive or unfocused text makes the examiner start yawning, glancing at his watch and then thinking about the word count.

There is one other, less formal reason to stick to the word count. A good project is an interesting project. One that is lively, clear and thoughtful. Long projects become dull to read and hard to follow. Psychologically, you are more likely to get the examiner on your side by being interesting than by being dull.

So how do you make sure you produce a good, analytic project with the right level of depth, while keeping the word count down. There are five key points to remember:

1   **Set clear objectives from the start.** Most projects wander because students start without clear objectives. So they follow a few trails: analyse the accounts, carry out a customer/staff survey and then

wonder what to do with it all. Eventually they decide on their objectives, and squeeze their findings in, pretending that they meet the project objectives. This leads to an excess of irrelevant material.

2   **Be ruthless at pruning background information.** You need to start by gaining a full understanding of your business and its marketplace. That does not mean that you need to reproduce all this data for the examiner. Above all else, make sure that you only include background material which relates directly to your project objectives and method.

3   **Good marks come from showing a skill, not from showing it repeatedly.** You may need to carry out market research to discover some essential information. Done well, this can generate many marks. Yet some students carry out two or even three surveys (or claim they have, anyway). There is virtually no scope for generating extra marks through the repetition of a technique. So plan your project method with care, ensuring that techniques are not repeated.

4   **Edit, rewrite, then re-edit.** In publisher-speak, 'slash and burn!' The psychology of project-writing is clear. You start by writing too much, by padding out sentences and paragraphs attempting to meet this apparently huge target of 3000 words. Later you realise you have written 7000 and cannot bear to delete words you have spent so long writing. But you must, your mark depends on it. Reread your background, method and so on. You will find it wordy and boring. Edit, re-write, then re-edit. If someone else will read it for you and point out especially woolly passages, welcome their attentions.

5   **Do not skimp on conclusions.** Students tend only to notice the excessive length of their work when they near the end of the report, by which time there is little more to do than smarten it up and write a conclusion. Now, no one likes writing conclusions, so there is a great temptation to say, 'Well, I've already written 5000 words, so I'll just do a brief conclusion.' Yet the Edexcel coursework marking criteria allocate 25% of the total mark to synthesis and evaluation – both skills which are tightly bound up in your recommendations and conclusions. It is crazy, therefore, to skimp on conclusions; prune the early part of the report, not the key later parts.

# 16.4 Internally assessed but externally moderated

With this assignment your teachers have to mark all the projects from your school/college. If there is more than one class studying Edexcel Business Studies, staff must agree on a single list of marks across all the classes. For this to occur, each teacher has not only to read and mark all the projects from their own class, but those from other classes too. This is a very time-consuming (and stressful) process. Therefore it is important that you should make sure to complete your report by the deadline set by staff.

Internal assessment has other implications for you. Teachers are inevitably influenced by the effort you have put in. They look to reward those who have researched thoroughly and honestly, and those who have worked hard on editing, re-writing and on presentation. If projects are marked externally, there is a greater chance that last-minute, largely invented work will slip past the unsuspecting examiner. Internal assessment gives you no hiding place. This leads to an inevitable conclusion: work hard, work early, involve your teacher, accept the advice given and make sure you meet deadlines. Good projects come from healthy cooperation between student and teacher/mentor.

A
B
C
D
E
F
G
H
I
J
K
L
M
N
O
P
Q
R
S
T
U
V
W
X
Y
Z

# Carrying out a feasibility study

A feasibility study is an investigation into the financial viability of a business proposal. In this context it is a study of whether a new business could be successful. Students usually carry out a feasibility study when they have no direct business contact to draw from and so need a project which can be researched independently.

## 17.1 Where to start

The starting point is usually an idea for a new business. Often this stems from a thoughtful look at (or analysis of) your local area. Is the district lacking a photo processing outlet, a shoe repair/key cutter or a Pizza Hut? If so, perhaps it is time one opened up. Or is there a new idea which could be marketed, such as a video rental shop with computer touch-screens on which you could, for instance, find all the films made by De Niro, plus a synopsis of the plot?

A refinement on the above approach (looking for inspiration) is to map the local marketplace. This is easy to do with a market such as eating out. All you would need is *Yellow Pages*, a map and a pencil to plot each restaurant within your area. Use coloured pencils and you will be able to spot whether the north-east of your district lacks a kebab shop or a Thai restaurant, in which case you could start by researching which one would be more popular.

The alternative approach is to visit a business library. Secondary research analysis of a market may reveal gaps or emerging trends. This would have been the way to spot (several years ago) that the pizza takeaway was becoming big business, perhaps before it was known in your area.

A library might also hold a very useful publication called the *Franchise World Directory*. This has long lists of franchise opportunities available, any of which may give you an idea. For instance, there is 'Elms5', offering franchises to be the operator of 5-a-side football leagues. The listing states an investment cost of £7500, a working capital requirement of £4000 and a franchise fee of £4000. Year 1 turnover is projected to be £16,500 and full contact details are provided. Now, this may seem poor value to you, but the idea of running 5-a-side football leagues as a business may either interest you, or spark off another idea.

Good feasibility projects are based on good business ideas, so time spent at this stage is very worthwhile.

A weakness of feasibility studies is that they are almost always on service businesses. Unfortunately a project on starting up a manufacturing firm from scratch would be very difficult without inside information.

## 17.2  How to develop your idea

Once you have decided on a business idea, you have to develop it. Start by asking yourself these fundamental marketing questions:

- **Who is my product aimed at?**
- **Why should they buy from me?**
- **What is my unique sales proposition (USP)?**
- **How will I persuade customers to become regulars?**

Frequently students undertake assignments about starting up a clothes shop or a pizza restaurant without ever considering the key issues of target marketing, product differentiation and product excellence. Yet these are the key strategic thoughts.

Among the main ways of developing your marketing strategy are:

- **geographical mapping**
- **market mapping**
- **customer research**
- **customer contact research**
- **repeat purchase.**

## Geographical mapping

If your project is on opening up a café, nothing could be more important than a map showing where competitors are located. This, together with traffic flows, will give a clear idea of a suitable location. So:

1     go to a library for a good street plan

2     decide how to categorize the cafés locally (e.g. traditional, modern, young, other)

3     look up Café in *Yellow Pages* and the *Thomson Local*, then plot them on the map using a colour key to distinguish the category

4     analyse the map's implications, in terms of market gaps or location clusters (sometimes it is better to be where rivals are clustered, because that is where consumers head for).

## Market mapping

In addition to (or instead of) geographical mapping, market mapping can be invaluable. It is harder though, because it requires you to visit and make a judgement of the competition. If you go along to three or four cafés, you should start to see the key consumer criteria. For example, you might consider the key dimensions to be traditional/trendy and cheap/expensive. Visit all the cafés in your target district and plot them on a market map as shown below.

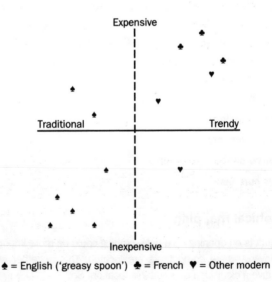

♠ = English ('greasy spoon')  ♣ = French  ♥ = Other modern

**Figure 17.1**

## Customer research

Within this heading comes the secondary research which may be needed to discover key information such as the age and income profile of consumers. This will be important to help you decide on the specifications and pricing of your product/service. If the age profile is quite old, for example, it may be that free delivery is a key factor. If young adults are the main age group, good parking facilities may be crucial.

Also available from secondary research sources are figures on market shares. These matter greatly, because if one firm dominates a market place it is probably unwise to devise a product which is comparable to theirs. It is safer by far to look for a highly distinctive niche.

## Customer contact research

Ideally you should decide on your marketing/product proposition through secondary research sources or the above two mapping exercises. A customer survey can then be conducted on the basis of a known proposition. Nevertheless there are some important details to learn about your local customers. For instance, if you have a contact at a retail outlet, you may be able to conduct a self-completion survey quite easily. Your questions could reveal information such as:

* **which rival outlets they visit, and why**
* **how highly they rate criteria such as location, range of products, price and parking when deciding where to shop/visit**
* **their likes and dislikes concerning this outlet.**

All this detail can help you present a logical case for the business proposition you are putting forward.

## Projects in Practice

Sonia's project was on opening an out of town music superstore in the Midlands with a wider range of titles than a Virgin Megastore and permanent discounts on the 'Top 10' singles and albums. Secondary data showed her the age profile of record buyers, which led to the uncomfortable conclusion that nearly half of all buyers of singles would be unable to drive to her store. She decided to conduct a survey among people who had bought something at the Walsall branch of Virgin (those carrying a Virgin plastic bag!). From this she was able to find out that her proposition was excellent. Furthermore, over half the 48% of respondents who could not drive felt confident that parents or friends would drive them to the store at least once a month.

If you have an entirely innovative product or service, it follows that no secondary research can exist. Therefore you may have to conduct a survey at this stage, to help formulate a target market and a clear consumer proposition. This is fine, but do remember that there is no value in conducting two market research exercises. So if you are also going to need a sales forecast, you must build the relevant questions into this same survey. (See Chapter 9 for further details.)

## Repeat purchase

In your product considerations and in market research, keep thinking about repeat business. No enterprise can survive for long without it. How exactly are you going to ensure that the repeat purchase level is high enough?

From a grading point of view this is a fruitful area for analysis. Try to distinguish the factors which determine initial trial from those which govern repeat purchase levels. For example, a special offer may encourage trial, but product/service quality will be far more important in determining long-term customer loyalty. If repeat purchase requires free parking or home delivery the costs can be built into the financial appraisal.

## 17.3 What financial data are needed for a feasibility study?

A feasibility study requires a decision to be made about whether or not a business enterprise is worth starting up. This can only be done convincingly if an appraisal method has been used, such as breakeven analysis, investment appraisal, a decision tree or projected accounts backed by ratio analysis. The most appropriate of these methods is investment appraisal. The following checklist applies to all four methods, though:

- **start-up costs**
- **sales revenue**
- **direct costs**
- **indirect overheads.**

## Start-up costs

These include:

- **cost of purchase/lease on premises**
- **legal and architects' fees for plans and planning permission**
- **building and decorating costs**
- **equipment cost and installation fees**
- **staff recruitment, training and uniforms**
- **cost of start-up stock level**
- **launch advertising/promotions.**

For each of these, it is important to obtain a timescale as well as costs. This will help with cash flow forecasting and/or critical path analysis.

## Sales revenue

Considerations include:

- **Forecast sales volume, in the short-, medium- and long-term (again, the timescale is very important).**
- **Planned price level (the same to all, or will you use some price discrimination or selective discounting?).**
- **Will sales be for cash or credit? This will affect the cash flow forecast.**
- **Are sales likely to be seasonal? Can an estimate of seasonal sales be built into the sales forecast (and therefore into variable costs and also the cash flow forecast).**

## Direct costs

These include:

* **materials/components/stocks bought in**
* **labour**
* **any other costs.**

(Note: these should be costs per unit, to be multiplied by the monthly sales forecast to give the costs/cash outflows.)

## Indirect overheads

These include:

* **rent and rates**
* **salaries and related costs**
* **expenses, e.g. electricity, phone, stationery, etc.**
* **interest charges**
* **depreciation (for profit and loss account and balance sheet only).**

Is this unmanageable? Well, almost. Yet students are able to find out most of this information. Typical sources are shown below.

### Possible sources of cost information for feasibility studies

| Costs involved | Possible source of information |
| --- | --- |
| Cost of purchase/lease of premises | estate agent with commercial arm |
| Rent and rates | estate agent or (for rates) the local council |
| Building and decorating | difficult without contact with a builder or the owner of a comparable shop |
| Equipment and installation | equipment suppliers; for contact details see trade press or directory or attend a trade exhibition |
| Staff recruitment, training and uniforms | for recruitment costs see local paper advertising rates in *BRAD*; for training course and uniforms see trade press or exhibitions |

| Start-up stock level | divide your expected annual cost of sales by the sector average stock turnover ratio (see *Key Financial Ratios*); this will give your stock level at a point in time |
| --- | --- |
| Launch advertising and promotions | see *BRAD* |
| Materials/components/ Stocks bought in | calculate through the % gross margin given in *Key Financial Ratios*, e.g. if gross margin is 30%, then 70% of sales revenue must be cost of sales |
| Labour and salary costs | see local paper recruitment ads and/or visit local job centre |
| Expenses | hard without advice from a comparable firm (note, though, that these costs are usually small, so a rough estimate of £1000 or so would not be automatically condemned) |
| Interest charges | calculate on the basis of any loans needed to start up the business |
| Depreciation | estimate the useful lifetimes of the fixed assets concerned, including the fixtures and fittings |

A B C D E F G H I J K L M N O P Q R S T U V W X Y Z

## Projects in Practice

Matthew's study into opening a nightclub estimated that the start-up costs would amount to £875,000 (even though the site was to be rented not purchased!). The costs included building, lighting, sound system, IT system, security system, bar equipment and staff uniforms. Worse, first year costs would amount to £992,000 compared with revenues estimated at £857,000. Fortunately, from then on rising revenues would move ahead of costs.

**Continued**

A summary of his complex calculations:

**In £000**

| | Year | | | | | |
|---|---|---|---|---|---|---|
| | **1** | **2** | **3** | **4** | **5** | **6** |
| Cash inflows | 857 | 1,240 | 1,364 | 1,501 | 1,650 | 1,815 |
| Initial outlay | 875 | | | | | |
| Annual operating outflow | 990 | 1,040 | 1,085 | 1,131 | 1,185 | 1,242 |
| Annual net cash flow | -1,008 | 200 | 279 | 370 | 465 | 573 |
| Cumulative cash flow | -1,008 | -808 | -529 | -159 | 306 | 879 |

This was converted into the graph shown below to give a visual summary of the information.

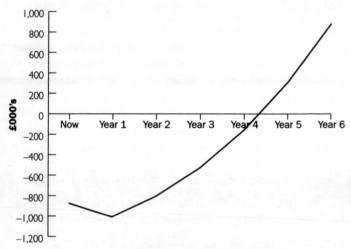

The graph helped illustrate that payback would occur after 52 months. And that although the average rate of return was 'only' 16.7%, the graph implied prospects for further, substantial profits in year 7 and beyond.

## 17.4 How important are the practical considerations?

Key practical issues in setting up a business include:

● **deciding which type of business organisation is appropriate (e.g. sole trader or private limited company)**

● **legal considerations such as planning permission, health and safety, and insurance**

● **how the finance can be raised**

● **the availability of a suitable site.**

The best general advice is to leave most of these points to one side. They often lead to descriptive work which is largely based upon text books. The only one which may yield some valuable analysis marks from a business studies examiner is the issue of sources of finance. Even here, though, there are many pitfalls. Students wanting to back up their feasibility study sometimes suggest that they have access to finance because of a legacy, savings (!) or (worst of all) because they have won the National Lottery.

Two approaches to the raising of finance which have been impressive are:

1 **Visit a bank manager or small business advisor, equipped with your nearly complete feasibility study. Show a summary of your work and discuss the terms on which the bank might consider lending some start-up capital. Your account of the conversation will make an interesting section within your project report.**

2 **An unconventional approach to raising finance can make interesting reading. A project by an Indian student gave an insider's view into the informal way in which family and friends would be likely to support a well-argued business case and gave a full account of the rewards that would be expected in return. The insights provided into a different business culture made high marks inevitable.**

## 17.5 How do you get high marks on a feasibility study?

Four main factors determine your grade with this type of project:

● **the quality of your research method and execution**

● **the depth of analysis you apply to your material**

● **the clarity of your communication**

● **how well you evaluate the work you have done.**

**169**

## The quality of your research method and execution

Tutors and examiners cannot help respecting hard work. If you have tracked down lots of detailed information from estate agents, builders, suppliers, consumers and so on, your project will impress. Other candidates will be submitting work containing figures plucked, apparently, from thin air, so it is very important that you should explain exactly how you obtained your data.

Hard work alone cannot be sufficient for top grades, however. The marks gained from your method will also depend upon:

* **the quality of the written justification of your approach**
* **the extent to which your method raises theoretical issues**
* **the range of sources you draw from.**

If, for example, you find out the detailed costs and revenues from an existing shop and use them as a cash flow forecast for your own shop, you may have lots of good data, but the process has required little from you. This is why it is useful to use techniques such as research surveys where relevant, especially if they can be used in conjunction with secondary data, as shown in Section 11.1.

## The depth of analysis you apply to your material

In carrying out a feasibility study, depth of analysis can be shown in many ways. In the above Projects in Practice box, the graph of cumulative cash when opening a nightclub gave scope for several telling points about financing, cash flow and the artificiality of calculating ARR over a six year period. All this came from the student's willingness to think about an interesting way to present the information.

Analysis in depth is likely to stem from excellent knowledge and understanding of the techniques being used. Therefore, before using a technique such as investment appraisal or critical path, make sure to read about it. Go beyond your class notes by looking for more demanding books; Appendix 2 gives you a useful starting point.

Think about the figures you are dealing with. Are there any patterns, any correlations, any figures which contradict others? Considering why one piece of evidence contradicts another is often a fruitful form of analysis.

Analysis marks are gathered most easily by applying numerical techniques such as breakeven analysis. Top marks for analysis come from looking further, perhaps by applying a more advanced approach (e.g. complex breakeven) or by writing a full, sceptical account of the method and its pitfalls.

## The clarity of your communication

This is a particular problem with feasibility studies, where the volume of data can swamp the flow of the report. Among the main features to consider are:

**1 Contents page.**

**A good contents page is a rare but invaluable item. It can be completed only after the whole structure of the project is clear. The following one from the nightclub project gives a good idea of the level of detail that is desirable.**

CONTENTS

| | | |
|---|---|---|
| Project structure and objectives | | 1–2 |
| <u>Market Analysis</u> | | |
| 1.1 | Analyse the current market place in Croydon to see if there is a gap in the market | 3–5 |
| 1.2 | Evaluation of findings to draw up any sources of product differentiation | 6–8 |
| <u>Financial feasibility</u> | | |
| 2.1 | To statistically test my questionnaire and estimate a percentage of the target market as actual users | 9–11 |
| 2.2 | To forecast demand for the dance club | 12 |
| 2.3 | To adjust the anticipated demand levels to incorporate industry trends | 13–14 |
| 2.4 | To forecast of sales turnover for first years operation | 15–16 |
| 2.5 | Estimation of stock levels and value | 17–19 |
| 2.6 | To estimate start up and on going costs | 20–26 |
| 2.7 | Process the figures in objective 2.4 and 2.6 into a cash flow forecast | 27–28 |
| 2.8 | Conduct a full investment appraisal | 29–32 |
| 2.9 | Produce a predicted profit and loss account for the first 7 years trading | 33–34 |
| <u>Conclusion and evaluations</u> | | |
| 3.1 | Will the project succeed to produce profit in the long term | 35–36 |
| 3.2 | Evaluation of the whole project | 37 |
| APPENDIX A: BIBLIOGRAPHY | | |
| APPENDIX B: REFERENCES | | |
| APPENDIX C: RAW DATA | | |

**Figure 17.2** Contents page example for nightclub report

2   Visuals linked to text.

The issue here is a simple one; full page tables or graphs may look good, but they rarely work. Unless they are self-explanatory the reader finds it difficult to interpret the information. It is far better to place graph and text on the same page. The result is a visually interesting page and far better communication.

3   Provide regular summaries of your arguments and conclusions.

4   Link the summaries to the objectives they meet.

5   Highlight the key data.

Feasibility studies tend to hinge on one key piece of analysis (often a cash flow forecast). It can be very effective to highlight its central importance, by making it a large, foldout double page.

6   Use of appendices.

The key to successful communication while keeping within the word limit is to use appendices appropriately. An appendix is a store of extra information or evidence which has been part of your decision making process. Reading this data is not essential to the flow of the report; indeed its details/figures may bog down the examiner. Yet it needs to be available both as proof that you did what you say you did and in case the reader wants more detail. A typical example of the use of an appendix is when analysing market research findings. The answers to key research questions should be shown and analysed within the body of the report. There may be other questions though, which can be displayed and interpreted in an appendix. You may mention the findings within the text, stating 'see Appendix X'. By convention, the words within appendices are not included within the word count total. Note, though, that examiners will not look through appendices unless they have been referred to within your text. Please note, also, that examiners hate to see appendices 'padded out' with company brochures, annual reports or other material of marginal relevance to your project.

Effective communication can be ensured only if you leave enough time after the completion of the text. At least a week will be needed, given the inevitability of rewriting some of the text to ensure that the structure you want is carried through effectively.

# Evaluation

A good example of evaluation was shown in Matthew's conclusions to his nightclub investment appraisal. He wrote:

> From my investment appraisal it would seem that my investment is financially sound. A payback period of 4.4 years seems long, but is only four months beyond the industry benchmark figure [he had explained this earlier]. Four years of negative cash flow will mean that substantial bank support will be needed in addition to attracting private investors. Fortunately the ARR of 17% is attractive, especially given that I used cautious assumptions at every stage in my cash flow forecasting. The net present value of +£450,000 is encouraging, but even since I calculated the figures using 6% discount factors the interest rates have risen by 0.25%. This highlights the criticism of NPV, that it assumes constant interest rates over long periods of time.

> Although the general conclusion must be positive, the investment appraisal results are only as good as the figures they are based on. Any inaccuracies in my sales forecast would have fed through into the cash flow forecast and then into the payback, ARR and NPV outcomes.

Note that this came in a section headed 'Summary and conclusions' which formed part of Matthew's report section 2.8, and was therefore an interim conclusion. Each of the other sections 2.1–2.9 contained an equivalent summary and conclusions while the full conclusion formed section 3. This approach verged on overkill, but showed full understanding of the relative importance of evaluation.

## 17.6 Summary and conclusion

A feasibility study can produce an excellent assignment. It forces you to undertake the types of research and analysis most likely to generate high marks. Examiners are inevitably won over by initiative, enterprise and hard work. A feasibility study is hardly possible without all of these components.

The following table provides a useful summary of how to conduct your study. The suggested word count should be taken only as a rough guide. It is based on a word count of 3500 words.

Useful academic starting points for a feasibility study include:

*Small Business Guide*, 16th Edition, Williams S.; Vitesse Media 2003. ISBN 0-9540812-4-2

*Starting your business*, Hingston, P.; Dorling Kindersley 2001. ISBN 0-7513-1413-7

| Stages in the project | Explanatory notes | Word count |
|---|---|---|
| Identify a business opportunity. | based on your own experience and interests | 75 |
| Analyse general market background. | secondary research such as *Mintel* | 300 |
| Analyse local market (consumers and competitors). | geographical mapping and/or market mapping | 475 |
| Decide how to make your business idea distinctive. | based on the above evidence | 100 |
| Gather the information to make a sales forecast. | from a survey and the 90/30 rule (see section 11.1) or from secondary sources such as *Key Financial Ratios* | 750 |
| Obtain cost information, then put together a cash flow forecast. | using your sales forecast and cost data | 500 |
| Analyse your information to help make a decision. | using investment appraisal, breakeven, decision trees or profit and loss accounts and balance sheet | 600 |
| Make recommendations about whether or not the proposal is worth pursuing. | use your quantified data, but make sure to evaluate it through qualitative factors such as risk | 200 |
| Make judgements about your project's findings and about the project process. | take your time here; draft and re-draft | 500 |

# A-Z Glossary of Business coursework

**Annual abstract of statistics:** a book of key economic and social statistics produced annually by the government. It is an important source of secondary data such as population figures and consumer expenditure trends. It is produced by the Office of National Statistics and available from The Stationery Office and most public and college libraries.

**annual report and accounts:** the document produced by the directors of a limited liability business to report to shareholders on the firm's financial performance and prospects. Public companies produce glossy, colourful reports and often make them publicly available through the (free) *Financial Times* annual report service. A public company's annual report provides:

* **a profit and loss account and balance sheet for the last two years**

* **a cash flow statement**

* **the chairman's report on future prospects**

* **the directors' report on current trading and policies.**

**appendices** are pages at the end of a document where you can place supporting evidence which is too bulky or detailed for the main body of text. Good use of appendices ensures that the reader/examiner is not bogged down or bored by page after page of numerical data or graphs. For example, you may have used a questionnaire containing ten questions. Only three of the questions provided important information for tackling the project objectives, so instead of trudging through all ten, the wise student puts the responses to seven of the questions in an appendix (making sure to tell the reader where they can be found). It is normal practice to exclude the appendices from the project's word count.

**assertion:** a statement which suggests or claims knowledge which is not supported by evidence. This may reveal prejudice (e.g. 'All women are …') or an inability to distinguish opinion from fact. Research assignments should be about gathering evidence upon which theories or argument can be based. Students who rely on unsupported assertions will never achieve high marks for method or analysis.

**assumptions** are the opinions or decisions which underlie the approach you take. They may be conscious (thought through) or unconscious. The key to a good project is to identify your assumptions and state them clearly. If, for example, you are working on a new product sales forecast, it may be essential to make an assumption about how competitors will respond. It does not matter what you assume, as long as you make your thinking clear to the reader/examiner.

**bias:** deflection from the truth due to an individual's self-interest or a faulty research method. For students, there are two main types of bias to consider:

1  **biased views, for example when managers talk about their own leadership style most claim to be democratic, yet their staff may have a very different view; top projects obtain a variety of views, so that bias can be identified**

2  **research bias is far harder to deal with; if you interview 50 pub goers, how can you know whether their views are representative and accurate; perhaps they are being 'helpful' to you by giving positive responses; all you can do is to keep alert for possible sources of bias and discuss them in your findings.**

**bibliography:** a list of your written research sources such as books, newspapers, annual accounts or leaflets. They should be provided in detail, with the author name, the publisher and the date of publication. A bibliography impresses examiners only if its contents have been referred to directly within the text of the report. It is good practice, therefore, to give the occasional direct quote, such as:

> 'Jewell's definition of forecasting is 'an attempt to predict the future behaviour of a variable' (see Jewell, 3rd edition, Longman, 1997)'

Then the inclusion of full details of the book in your bibliography becomes academically worthwhile.

**British Rate and Data (BRAD)** provides contact details and advertising costs for every newspaper, magazine, radio and TV station in the UK. It also provides similar details on many web sites that sell advertising space. This makes it invaluable for project work. If your assignment is on a cleaning company, a look under the letter C will reveal a number of relevant trade magazines. Later, once you have decided on a new marketing strategy, BRAD enables you to see how much an advertising campaign will cost.

**CCH Business Focus** provides wonderful information for project work. Not only does it cover market information (e.g. 2002 market size for UK Hairdressing = £3.8 billion), but also costs of start-up and costs of operating. Available in some public libraries. Bigger schools and colleges could buy the full set of 90 trade sectors for just £250. Contact CCH Group Ltd. 145 London road, Surrey KT2 6BR.

**closed question:** a question to which a limited number of preset answers are offered, e.g. 'Do you buy a newspaper nowadays? Yes/No'.

**cluster sample:** sampling respondents drawn from a relatively small area selected to represent a particular aspect of a product's target market. For example, the cluster may be a seaside town chosen by a producer of sun lotion.

**Companies House** is where the Registrar of Companies holds financial and ownership data on every limited liability business. It has offices in Birmingham, Cardiff, Edinburgh, Glasgow, Leeds, London and Manchester (for contact details see pages 205–6), any of which can be visited to carry out a 'company search'. This provides a copy of all the information they hold, including recent accounts and details of share ownership. There are three ways of making a company search:

1   **In person, for a fee of £5.00 per company (this is much the best way, if you live near to the above cities).**

2   **By phone, which must be to Cardiff; tel. 029 2038 0801 (or fax 029 2038 0517).**

3   **By post, to PO Box 709, Companies House, Crown Way, Maindy, Cardiff CF14 3UZ.**

Note that a helpful starting point for information is the Companies House website, www.companieshouse.gov.uk. Very usefully, this allows you to check that the company name you have is actually on their database, which can save a wasted journey. It also provides a latest price list and the opportunity to order a company search by email.

**confidentiality:** the real or imagined need to keep information secret from those outside the company. Large companies are likely to be concerned that competitors or the press might obtain the data. Family businesses may want to prevent someone they know from finding out their wealth (balance sheet) or earnings (profit and loss account). Project writers should remember that the company name can always be changed, to help maintain confidentiality, and if necessary, a note can be written at the start of the project asking for complete confidentiality from the reader/examiner. Before agreeing a working title it is sensible to check with a project contact that the information will not be too confidential to be seen by an examiner.

**confidence levels** are yardsticks for deciding whether market research findings have the accuracy to allow meaningful conclusions to be drawn. Professional market researchers usually look for a 95% confidence level, in other words sufficient accuracy for the results to be right 19 times out of 20. This is achieved if the finding is reliable to two standard deviations.

**Consumer Goods UK** (formerly Retail Business) is a useful source of market intelligence, focusing each month on different retail markets. It is published by Retail Intelligence, 48 Bedford Square, London WC1B 3DP, tel. 020 7814 3814.

**convenience sampling** means interviewing those who happen to be available. This is the very opposite to scientific approaches such as random sampling, and raises serious concerns about sampling bias. In practice, though, it may be the only approach open to a project writer. If you are using convenience sampling, be especially careful to consider the issue of sampling bias.

**correlation** measures links which might exist between two or more sets of numerical data. Highly correlated data would form a predictable pattern, such as that for every £100 extra spent on advertising, sales rise £500. If the correlation is total, the data will form a straight line on a scatter graph. Correlation is a useful technique for project work; see section 11.4.

**decision making model:** a formal procedure to ensure that decisions are arrived at in an objective manner. It attempts to eliminate hunch or bias by ensuring that decisions are based on factual, numerical evidence. Following a model such as the one below helps to improve a project's academic validity:

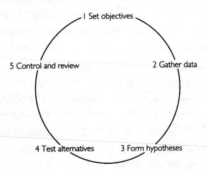

*Scientific decision-making model*

**EIU (Economist Intelligence Unit):** this is a major supplier of economic and business data with expertise in markets throughout the world. Bigger reference libraries are likely to hold the EIU country reports, which provide quarterly information on every economy in the world.

**evaluation:** judgements based on evidence. These may be made by drawing conclusions from the evidence presented throughout the project and/or as conclusions at the end. Typically, project conclusions look not only at the assignment's business lessons, but also at what the individual has learned from the process. (See Chapter 12 on conclusions.)

**evidence:** facts, figures or the views of others which lend support to your conclusions.

**Extel** supplies financial data on companies, either in written or electronic form. *Extel Company Research* (published by Financial Times Information) provides full published accounts for all quoted companies (those public companies listed on the Stock Exchange). If the library subscribes to the full service, *Extel Unquoted* also covers the larger public and private companies which are not on the stock market. Extel has now been renamed Sequencer.

**external moderation** means that the coursework will be examined by an external examiner, not someone from your own school or college. This makes it crucial that every aspect of the research method should be explained carefully for the examiner.

**extrapolation:** making a statistical forecast based on recent trends in the data. For example, if a school's pupil numbers have risen by 100 in each of the last three years, extrapolation would suggest another 100 will be added next year. Extrapolation can be used extensively in project work, with or without seasonal adjustments of the data.

Projects benefit from clear yardsticks against which results can be measured. Extrapolation is often a good way of providing such yardsticks. For example, if a firm's sales turnover in the last three years has been: three years ago £120,000; two years ago £114,000; last year £110,000, it is reasonable to project a figure of around £108,000 for next year, other things being equal. A project objective can therefore be to make recommendations which will push revenue above £108,000 (perhaps to £120,000).

**feasibility study:** an investigation into the likely profitability of a business proposition. This is usually followed up by recommending whether or not to proceed. Chapter 16 provides a full account of how to carry out a feasibility study.

**Financial Times Annual Reports Service:** a free service enabling investors and students to order the annual report and accounts for a wide range of public companies. The service even allows you to order all the reports from within a business sector such as food retailing – ideal for inter-firm ratio analysis. (Contact details: FT Annual Reports Service, Westmead House, 123 Westmead Road, Sutton, Surrey SM1 4JH, tel. 020 8391 6000, fax. 020 8391 9520.)

**footnotes:** explanatory notes put at the bottom of the page and referred to with an asterisk or superscript number at the end of a word or sentence. Within a project, the most likely use of footnotes is to provide a glossary of terms, especially if the company concerned uses its own jargon.

**forecasting:** predicting the future, either by statistical methods such as time series analysis, or through expert opinions (known as the Delphi method). The most common business functions in which forecasting is used are: economic forecasting, sales forecasting and cash flow forecasting. All three tend to be done on the basis of extrapolation, in other words projecting the future based upon past trends.

**Franchise World Directory** is an annual publication giving details of available franchise businesses. It provides full details of franchise fees, the start-up capital required and the projected annual turnover. It is published by *Franchise World* magazine at James House, 37 Nottingham Road, London SW17 7EA, tel 020 8767 1371.

**glossary:** an alphabetical listing of the definitions of words used in your project which may not be known to your examiner. There is no need to define standard business terms such as 'depreciation'. It is very helpful, though, to explain words which are unique to the business you are dealing with, for example, what is a 'grill order'? (McDonald's jargon for a one-off order, e.g. for a Big Mac with no pickle.) What does 'I.T.1'? mean? (It is the trades union jargon for the form needed to apply to an industrial tribunal in an unfair dismissal case.)

**hypothesis:** a theory which can be tested through research. Projects are often based around the testing of a hypothesis. For example, having analysed a firm's strengths and weaknesses, you may believe that there is an opportunity for it to sell via the Internet. Your project can be a test of that hypothesis.

**investment appraisal:** forecasting the cash flows connected with an investment, then evaluating them through methods such as payback, average rate of return and discounted cash flow. In projects, it is helpful to discover whether the firm applies any criterion levels such as:

| Method | Criterion levels | |
|---|---|---|
| Payback period | Maximum | 2 years |
| Average rate of return | Minimum | 16% |
| Net present value | Minimum | 10% of initial outlay |

**Key Notes:** market intelligence reports into a variety of consumer markets, they are updated every year and for this reason they are often more up to date than rivals such as Mintel. Each Key Note report is focused on a specific market, such as chocolate confectionery or soft drinks. To see which public libraries stock Key Notes, see pages 196 and 197. An alternative is to visit the business library of your nearest university.

**MRGB:** see Market Research of Great Britain.

**Market Research of Great Britain (MRGB):** a monthly publication providing secondary data on consumer markets such as liqueurs, sunglasses or motorbikes. It is not as widely available as Mintel or Key Notes, but every bit as useful for market size, share and trend information – the typical background data for a project.

**McCarthy** is a business orientated press cuttings service. It supplies articles written on companies in the *Financial Times*, *Times*, *Observer*, *Economist* and over 40 other publications. This is ideal for background research on a company such as Sainsbury's. Several libraries have McCarthy's on CD-ROM, which makes it easier to track down particular issues or events by using key word searches.

**methodology:** the method you intend to use to achieve your objectives. This must include the academic justification for what you are doing, together with careful thought about any weaknesses in your method. A full account of project method is contained in Chapter 6.

**Mintel** is a leading provider of market intelligence information. Each year it analyses 120 consumer markets, looking at: market size and trends, market segmentation, the supply structure (competition), advertising and promotion, distribution, the consumer and the future including a market forecast. Examples of the sectors it covers are: make-up, vacuum cleaners, pizza and chocolate confectionery. Mintel is willing to supply a free index to its reports which will help you know whether it is worth your while to make the effort to visit a reference library which holds Mintel. (Contact details are: Mintel International Group Ltd., 18–19 Long Lane, London EC1A 9HE, tel. 020 7606 4533, fax. 020 7606 5932.)

**Ninety/thirty rule (90/30 rule):** an American researchers' rule of thumb to help translate market research findings into market share predictions. The rule is that 90% of those saying 'Will definitely buy regularly' plus 30% of those saying 'Will very probably buy regularly' should end up buying the product. The risk with the rule is that it can lead to some improbably high sales forecasts.

**objectives** are targets which must be achieved if an overall aim is to be achieved. Having set out the project objectives, a student can decide on the appropriate methods for achieving them.

**observation:** gathering information by watching and recording what happens. This is a good way of obtaining unbiased, quantified data. Examples include:

- **measuring how many pedestrians walk past two potential shop sites**

- **observing how customers move around a shop; which parts they visit and which they avoid**

- **watching the progress of an order as it moves from design to manufacture and assembly.**

**open questions** are those that invite a wide-ranging, reflective or imaginative response. On a questionnaire, they are questions that do not have specific answers to be ticked. They therefore require the respondent to take the time to write out (or explain verbally) their answer. This is time consuming, but has the huge advantage of generating actual answers which can be quoted directly in your report. Tick-box answers can never provide the impact of a direct answer such as 'I was disgusted by the rotting strawberries in the punnets' (a written answer to a general question about the quality of service at a village grocers).

**piloting a questionnaire** means testing it out on a few people before finalizing the questions. In this way questions which are unclear can be identified and changed. Postal surveys are expensive to carry out, so it makes sense to test the questionnaire before sending out dozens.

**primary research** means gathering first-hand data that is tailor-made to a firm's own products, customers or markets. Primary research is carried out by fieldwork, whereas secondary (second-hand) data is gathered by desk research. Chapter 9 gives a full account of how to handle primary research.

**pro forma accounts** are forecast accounts for the first year or two of a new business. The main accounts are the balance sheet and profit and loss account. Pro forma accounts are important when conducting a feasibility study.

**questionnaire:** a document containing a series of questions designed to discover the information required to meet your research objectives. When writing questionnaires there are four main principles to bear in mind:

- **each question should ask only one point**
- **questions should not contain bias (e.g. 'How much do you like cider?')**
- **the time, cost and ability to quantify the analysis of the answers depend on whether the questions are closed or open; closed questions are far more common (e.g. 'Have you bought cider within the last week?' Yes/No)**
- **the questions must be asked in the right sequence, leaving personal details such as age, address and occupation until the end, and making sure that earlier questions do not bias the answers to later ones.**

**quota sampling:** the recruitment of respondents to a market research exercise in proportion to their known demographic profile. If you know that 25 per cent of your buyers are men, you would instruct interviewers to recruit one man for every three women within your sample. This is a far quicker and usually more effective method than random sampling.

**random sampling:** contacting survey respondents so that every member of the population has an equal chance of being interviewed. This sounds straightforward but is, in fact, both hard and expensive to achieve. The reason is that random must not be confused with haphazard. If all you did was to stand outside Marks & Spencer one Tuesday afternoon and interview as many people as necessary, various distortions would occur in the sample:

- **relatively few men would be interviewed**
- **few working women would be interviewed**
- **few hardworking students would be interviewed.**

In other words, the sample would be biased towards pensioners, parents of preschool children and the unemployed.

In order to avoid these pitfalls, random samples are drawn from local electoral registers, and interviewees are contacted at home. The interviewer should call three times before giving up on an address, to overcome the problem that busy people are the least likely to be at home. The need to visit and revisit specific addresses adds considerably to the time involved in fieldwork so this method is very unlikely to be used in an A level project.

**rationale:** a careful explanation of the reasoning behind a recommendation or decision. A project might, therefore, have a recommendations section broken down into 'recommendations' and 'rationale'.

**reliability of research findings** is a key issue. Sample findings can only be reliable if the sampling method is accurate, the research method unbiased and the sample large enough to generate statistically valid data. It is always sensible to comment on the reliability of your own primary research, taking care to avoid firm recommendations if the reliability is low.

**research assignment:** a term used by OCR (the Cambridge Board), meaning a project/coursework. It should be based upon primary and secondary research and presented as a report.

**response rate:** the proportion of respondents contacted who reply to the questions asked. A low response rate might mean biased findings if, for example, non-respondents had different views from those who did respond. This is a problem with postal surveys, where response rates may be as low as 20%. Are the missing 80% just lazy, or are they not replying because they are not interested in your product/service? As long as a student draws conclusions from the response rate achieved, marks can be gained whether the response level is high or low.

**sample size:** the number of interviews carried out within a survey. In research assignments, the key is to ensure a large enough sample size to enable meaningful conclusions to be drawn. This requires either statistical reliability (which can be achieved with samples of 50+) or a high proportional sample. An example of the latter would be interviewing 25 of the 50 staff employed within a workplace. The only exception to these 'rules' is if your method includes street interviewing. This is so time consuming that a sample of 25 might be an impressive achievement. A very rough guide to acceptable sample sizes would be:

- **self-completion surveys within a controlled area (e.g. at school/ college): sample = 100**
- **face to face interviewing in the workplace: sample = 25+ or 50%+**
- **face to face street interviewing: sample = 25+.**

**secondary research** involves collecting information from second-hand sources such as reference books, government statistics or market intelligence reports. These sources can provide information on market size and market trends for most product categories. It may be accessible publicly and therefore free, but is in any case not as expensive to gather as primary data. Secondary research is considered fully in Chapter 8.

**sensitivity analysis:** calculating the sensitivity of financial forecasts to changes in the underlying assumptions. For example, your best estimates of a new project's costs and revenues may lead you to forecast a two year payback on an investment. But what if the selling price had to be cut by 10%; What might the payback be now? If payback were now after four years the firm might decide the investment is too marginal to be worth proceeding with.

**situational audit:** an impartial check on the circumstances faced by an existing, or new, business. For example, an entrepreneur thinking of opening an internet café in Stockport would check on the number of competitors, the number of students living locally and the cost of property in the different possible sites.

**Snapshots** calls itself The Complete Market Research Toolbox. It comes as a CD Rom and is available in many of the bigger public libraries. It offers data on a huge range of markets, e.g. UK Garden Products Retailing and UK Hotels. If you were considering starting up a hotel, it would provide you with data on the 2002 UK market size (£8,839,000) and the number of hotels in the UK (48,171), enabling you to work out the average sales revenue per hotel. It also provides data on market trends and shares.

**sources:** a clear statement of where information comes from. This is essential if your work is to have academic credibility. So state exactly where your secondary data came from or who provided you with the criticism of the business's management style.

If the source was a textbook, it is unacceptable to pretend that you wrote it; this is known as 'plagiarism' and is regarded as a serious form of cheating. Moderators are impressed by projects based upon wide reading, backed by clear reference to sources; there is no need to pretend.

**stratified sample:** a research sampling method that draws respondents from a specified subgroup of the population. An example would be a project on marketing a new premium lager. You might decide to research solely among 18–30-year-old men, since they represent the heart of that marketplace. Within the chosen group, individuals might be chosen on a random basis, hence the term 'stratified random sample'.

**trade association:** an organisation which represents the industry in negotiations with government and often acts as a central store of resources on an industry or sector. For example, a student doing a project on opening an ice skating rink would surely like to know that there is a National Ice Skating Association of UK Ltd. Contact details could be found in the directory *Trade Associations and Professional Bodies of the United Kingdom*, available at larger libraries.

**trade magazines/papers** are the press media produced for a specialized business audience; included are magazines such as *The Grocer* or *Off Licence News*. These publications are valuable sources of secondary information. Here you might find an article on a new off licence which has proved particularly profitable, or advertisements by suppliers of shop fittings or other equipment. Such information might be very useful indeed. To find out the relevant trade magazine for you, look in the index of *British Rate and Data* (BRAD), available in most public libraries.

**traffic count:** a physical count of the cars or pedestrians passing a specified site. This can be very useful when forecasting sales for a new outlet. For example:

|  | **Passing cars per hour** | **Annual sales** |
| --- | --- | --- |
| Existing KFC drive-thru, Coventry | 1500 | £1.20 m (actual) |
| Proposed new KFC drive-thru, Wolverhampton | 1800 | £1.44 m (forecast) |

**unique selling point (USP):** this marketing term should never be forgotten when undertaking coursework. What is your assignment's USP? It is the special feature which will make the examiner sit up and take notice. It might be a particularly clever visual idea, or some really interesting data (such as the profit margins on Big Macs and Shakes).

**value judgement:** an opinion which is not supported by evidence. Value judgements are often stated as if they are facts, for example 'northerners are lazier than southerners' (or vice versa!). This type of writing is far removed from the academic approach required in business projects.

**word limit:** the approximate maximum word count allowed by the exam board. This does not include tables of figures or appendices, so it can be misleading to use the word count facility on word processing software.

**Z-score:** the proportion of outcomes within a specified part of a normal distribution, measured in terms of standard deviations. The z-score enables statistical significance to be measured with more precision than just in terms of one, two or three standard deviations.

A
B
C
D
E
F
G
H
I
J
K
L
M
N
O
P
Q
R
S
T
U
V
W
X
Y
Z

# A–Z of resources for business coursework

This resource section of the handbook is organised into six sections. Each provides you with ways of obtaining the information, and possibly contacts, you need to produce a top grade project. It will pay dividends if you browse through this section. Ideas may be sparked off that would not have come spontaneously. After all, how can you think about something you did not know existed?

This section consists of:

1 **How to research into ...**

2 **The Internet**

3 **Libraries**

4 **Books**

5 **Organisations**

6 **Other sources of data**

## 1 How to research into ...

## COMPANY ACCOUNTS

The accounts for all limited companies can be tracked down. For public limited companies, it may be as simple as phoning the firm for a copy of the annual report, or using the excellent *Financial Times Annual Reports Service*. Private limited companies can also be looked into, as they all have to supply their accounts annually to Companies House. Every member of the public has the right to look at the accounts and the firm itself cannot know who has been looking.

Unfortunately there is no way to find the accounts of the majority of businesses which are unlimited (ones that do not say Ltd or plc after the company name). So, if your project concerns an unlimited liability firm, the only way you can get the accounts is from your project contact.

The references made below relate only to firms with Ltd (private limited company) or plc (public limited company) after their names.

For full details on key sources and addresses, see pages 204–8.

# EXPORT SALES AND MARKETING

*EIU Country Reports:* quarterly publications, one per country, from Australia to Zambia. Each provides statistics on economic trends, planned changes in laws and taxes and forecasts of future trends in exchange rates, inflation and economic activity.

*European Marketing Data and Statistics 2000* provides data on population changes and projections, economic indicators, consumer expenditure, retailing and distribution, advertising spending, per capita consumption figures and labour force indicators. This is the book to come to for data such as 'breakfast cereal consumption per year: Britain 7.2 kg, Sweden 0.4 kg', or how many hypermarkets there are in France! (Published by Euromonitor plc.)

**Eurostat Publications** provide a variety of economic and other statistical information on the countries of the European Union. They are worth contacting at the Office of Official Publications of the European Union, The Stationery Office, PO Box 276, London SW8 5DT, tel. 0870 600 5522.

**Market Research Europe** provides monthly analyses of a wide range of markets. Some reports are Europe-wide, such as recent ones on soft drinks in Europe, CDs and stationery. In addition there are reports on specific markets within individual countries, for example fast food in France (published by Euromonitor plc).

*Monthly Bulletin of Statistics,* United Nations, is a booklet full of figures about countries throughout the world. It is useful for data such as population trends, industrial output, inflation and exchange rates. A useful aspect is that it is likely to be held by almost every reference library.

# THE IDEAL FINANCIAL STRUCTURE FOR A BUSINESS START-UP

Look carefully at the following publications, any of which may be available at a business oriented reference library or at a university library:

*Industrial Performance Analysis* provides very similar information to *Key Financial Ratios*, though with less detail (published by ICC Business Ratios).

**Jordan's *Britain's Top Privately Owned Companies*** gives full details of the top 10,000 private companies. These may include firms you know to be successful in the specific market you're interested in, such as KFC UK Ltd or McDonald's UK Ltd.

*Key Financial Ratios:* this is a marvellous source of data on good, average and poor accounts for firms in every type of business. For example, in the category 'music and record retailing' gross profit margins average 36%, but net margins are only 1.4%; stocks account for 48% of total assets and while the average return on capital is 6.3%, the best performing quarter of companies make 32.1% while the poorest performers average −13.5%. See section 8.4 for further details on how to use this resource (published by Dun and Bradstreet).

**Kompass** *Financial Data* provides a similar service to Jordan's; it covers 30,000 firms but in less detail.

**Waterlow's** *Unquoted Companies* covers 20,000 firms with very full accounting information. It is at least as useful as Jordan's.

## 2 The Internet

Ask your college library if they can get hold of a book called 'Free Business and Industry Information on the Web' by Paul Pedley, published by Astib-IMI. The author's website is worth visiting: www.paulpedley.com

| Website | Internet address | What the site can provide |
|---|---|---|
| **BBC Online** the BBC's massive website | http:// www.bbc.co.uk | Great for the latest stories and data, though I much prefer Google |
| **Benchmark Index** a website sponsored by the government (DTI) to promote its 1996 Benchmark Index initiative | http:// benchmarkindex. com | Helpful for ordering the Benchmark Journal; also there's a facility to benchmark on-line, i.e. find out how your contact firm compares with others |
| **BizEd on the Net** is the website set up specifically for teachers and students of A level business and economics | http://bized.ac.uk | Most useful aspect of this site is access to a limited form of Extel data (company accounts); the site also gives ONS data (govt. stats.) |

**Business link** is the government funded network of over 200 advice centres for small to medium sized businesses

http://www.businesslink.co.uk

Provides advice on starting up, expanding or bench--marking a business; provides contact details of the branch nearest to you

**Central Office of Information:** the government department responsible for communication and information

http://www.coi.gov.uk

A useful starting point for latest government information, e.g. response to a crisis

**Chambers of commerce:** local groups of business--people who meet to discuss issues of concern (e.g. the need for a new motorway)

http://www.brainstorm.co.uk/BCC

Contact details of the 52 chambers of commerce; useful if you want the wider business view on a local issue; also focuses upon exporting for small firms

**Companies House:** where information is kept on all limited companies, including accounts and details of shareholdings

http://www.companieshouse.gov.uk

Allows you to check a company name against their database; provides a latest price list and the opportunity to order a company search by email

**Confederation of British Industry (CBI):** the main employers' organisation in the UK

http://www.cbi.org.uk

Contact to obtain details of their 13 regional offices

**Department of Trade and Industry (DTI):** the government department responsible for promoting business needs, growth and exports

http://www.dti.gov.uk

Useful pages on 'business support' include details of export services, regional selective assistance, loan guarantee scheme and much else; also has excellent links to other government sites

A B C D E F G H I J K L M N O P Q R S T U V W X Y Z

| | | |
|---|---|---|
| **European Union (and Eurostat):** the main website for the EU and its statistics arm, Eurostat | http://europa. eu.int | Good for up to date facts and figures, useful for latest changes in laws or the single currency |
| **Financial Times website:** an easily accessible goldmine of data on companies, especially plcs | http://www. ft.com | Very up to date, providing all articles on companies during the last month, both in the FT and in media worldwide. A trawl for Nokia found 57 FT articles, 3658 from elsewhere and 117,519 'relevant' websites! |
| **Google:** probably the best general search engine | http:// www.google.co.uk | Put in any company name and it is likely to provide lots of information |
| **Incomes Data Services:** the website for the prestigious research company that specialises in pay (including top people's pay) | http://www. incomesdata.co.uk | Super site for researching into remuneration: pay, fringe benefits, performance-related pay, share options, etc. |
| **HM Treasury:** the Chancellor of the Exchequer's website | http://www. hm-treasury. gov.uk | Provides a useful 'economic overview', with latest economic data updated weekly; useful for full details of latest budget |
| **Office for National Statistics (ONS):** the UK government's provider of statistical information | http://www. statistics.gov.uk | Shows exactly which publications are available from the ONS, contact details etc.; little free data to be found, unfortunately |

**Thompson Directory:** the business contact directory is on the Internet, which makes it easy for you to obtain names and addresses, e.g. for postal surveys

http://www. thomson-directories co.uk

If your project is on a company making fruit machines, this site could be used to identify the addresses of 100 pubs in the UK, for a postal survey

**Trades Union Congress (TUC):** the body representing most trades unions in UK

http://www. tuc.org.uk

Provides the union's views on issues such as the minimum wage; gives access to other union sites, such the as those of GMB and Unison

## 3 Libraries: marketing resources in UK libraries

Surprisingly, there is no national register to show which library holds what. So the following table is unique. It was produced by writing to 50 of the largest public libraries in the UK chosen to give as wide a geographic spread as possible, so that no one is too far from a library with some useful resources.

Forty-seven libraries were kind enough to respond, although a few took some prodding. The achievement of such a high response rate shows how co-operative libraries are.

Several librarians wrote to point out that budget cutbacks occur regularly so the fact that these resources were held in early 1998 does not mean they will necessarily be available in future. Many also made it clear that they do not hold all Mintel or Key Note reports, therefore it is wise to phone in advance before making a long journey. The contact details, including phone and fax are given after the table.

In addition to the marketing and business resources listed in the table below, all these libraries (and many others) can be expected to hold the main sources of government statistical data: *Economic Trends*, the *Monthly Digest of Statistics*, *Social Trends* and *Labour Market Trends*.

The librarians also pointed out that they have other local and national marketing resources of value. So do not only look for the secondary sources listed below; ask for further assistance. Most librarians have extraordinarily wide knowledge and their job is to answer questions.

The secondary resources referred to in the following table are:

**Consumer Goods UK:** another source of secondary market intelligence; the only one focusing on retail markets such as chemists.

**Consumer Trends:** useful for providing data on market size and market growth.

**Extel (now Sequencer):** provides up to date company accounts: profit and loss accounts and balance sheets.

**FT (1+ Year):** holds back numbers of the *Financial Times* for at least one year.

**Key Financial Ratios:** a goldmine of accounting ratios in different business sectors. If not available, alternatives are shown.

**Key Notes:** individual reports on different consumer markets, giving size, share, trends, etc.

**MRGB:** Market Research of Great Britain provides monthly updates on different consumer markets.

**McCarthy's:** a press cuttings service focusing on business and company news.

**Mintel:** market intelligence, giving even more detail than Key Notes.

**Pocket Books:** AC Nielsen publish an annual series of Pocket Books that contain a remarkable wealth of secondary data. For example, 'The Drink Pocket Book 2003' provides full data on market size, share, trends, advertising spending and consumer profile on consumers of beer, cider, wine, soft drinks and so on. Other very useful volumes include 'The Marketing Pocket Book', 'The Regional Pocket Market Book' and 'The Lifestyle Pocket Book'. Publisher: WARC, Farm Road, Henley-on-Thames, Oxfordshire RG9 1ET.

## The A-Z Guide to marketing research library resources

The libraries listed on pages 196–7 are among the best for business in the UK. Each entry shows the sources the library has available, with an indication of the quality of the material. The libraries have rated themselves into one of four categories, with 1 being the best.

Categories:

**1** **holds all copies**

**2** **good coverage of up-to-date volumes**

**3** **good coverage, but mainly 2–3 years old**

**4** **fair, but patchy provision.**

In the pages following the library listings, full contact details are provided for each library. Before travelling long distances to get to a library, it is wise to phone or fax first. If a local council cuts the library budget, subscriptions to expensive secondary business data can be cancelled.

**Notes:**
**Glasgow, Mitchell Library** offers free internet access and many other sources of secondary data.
**Cheltenham, Hull, Leeds** and **Truro** also have on-line access to Companies House records (there is a charge for this service)
**Southampton** holds A4 pages on setting up different types of business, e.g. Sports Shop

**Key:**
P = paper; E = electronic.

| Library | Mintel | Key Notes | Consumer Goods UK | MRGB | Consumer Trends | Key Financial Ratios | Extel | McCarthy | FT 1yr+ | Company Reports |
|---|---|---|---|---|---|---|---|---|---|---|
| **London & S.East** | | | | | | | | | | |
| Bedford Central | 2P+E | | | | | | | E | 5+ | 2 |
| City Business Library | 1 | 1 | 1 | 1 | 1 | FAME | 1E | 1E | 5+ | 2 |
| Colchester | | | | | | | 1E | 1E | 6 months | |
| Croydon Central | 1E | | | | | | | 1E | 5+ | 2 |
| Central Resources Hatfield | 1E | 1E | | | 1 | | | 1E | 10+ | 2 |
| London, British Library | 1 | 1 | 1 | | 1 | FAME | 1E | 1E | 10+ | 2 |
| **South & S. West** | | | | | | | | | | |
| Bath Central | | | | | | | | | 3 months | 4 |
| Bristol Central | 3 | 4 | 4 | 3 | | | | 1 | 5+ | 2 |
| Cheltenham Reference | 2 | 4 | | 3 | | | | | 5+ | 2 |
| Exeter Central | | 2P+E | | | | 2 | | | 3+ | 2 |
| Landsdowne, Bournemouth | 2 | | | | | | | | 1+ | |
| Oxford Central | | 2 | 1 | | 1 | | | 2E | 2+ | 2 |
| Reading | 1E | | | | | FAME | | | 15+ | |
| Southampton | 2 | 2 | 1 | | | ICC online | | 4 | 5+ | 2 |
| Truro | | 2 | | | | | | | 1+ | 2 |
| Winchester Reference | | 2 | | | | some | | | 20+ | 4 |
| **Midlands & E. Anglia** | | | | | | | | | | |
| Birmingham Central | 2 | 2E | 2 | 2 | 2 | | | 1E | 1+ | 2 |
| Cambridge Central | 2 | 1 | | 1 | | | | | 5+ | 2 |
| Chelmsford | 2 | 1 | | 1 | | | | 1E | 5+ | |
| Derby Central | | | | | | | | 2E | 1 | 2 |
| Leicester Central | | | | | 4 | | | 3E | 2+ | 4 |
| Norwich Information | 2E | 2E | | | | | | 2E | 1+ | |

| Library | Mintel | Key Notes | Consumer Goods UK | MRGB | Consumer Trends | Key Financial Ratios | Extel | McCarthy | FT 1yr+ | Company Reports |
|---|---|---|---|---|---|---|---|---|---|---|
| **N. West** | | | | | | | | | | |
| Carlisle | 1 | | | | | | | | 1+ | 2 |
| Ellesmere Port | 2 | 2 | 2 | | 2 | | | | 3 | 2 |
| Liverpool Central | 2 | 1 | | | 1 | | | 1E | 5+ | 2 |
| Manchester Central | 1 | 1 | 1 | 1 | 1 | ICC Ratios | | 1E | 10+ | 2 |
| **N. East** | | | | | | | | | | |
| Barnsley Central | 2 | 3 | 3 | 3 | | | | | 5+ | 4 |
| Bradford Central | | 3 | 3 | 3 | 1 | ICC Ratios | | 1E | 5+ | 2 |
| Durham Branch | | | | | | | | | 1+ | |
| Hartlepool Central | 2 | | | | | | | | | |
| Hull Central | 4 | 1 | 1 | 1 | 1 | FAME | | | 5+ | 2 |
| Leeds Central | 1 | 1 | 1 | | | FAME | | 1 | 1+ | 2 |
| Middlesbrough Central | 3 | 3 | | 3 | | | | | 10+ | |
| Newcastle Central | 2 | | 1 | 1 | 1 | FAME | | 1E | 5+ | 4 |
| **Wales** | | | | | | | | | | |
| Aberystwyth Public | | | 2 | | | | | | 1+ | |
| Cardiff Central | 3 | 3 | | | 1 | | | 3E | 2+ | 2 |
| National Library of Wales | 2 | 2 | 2 | | | 2 | 1 | | 1+ | |
| Newport, ONS | 2 | 1 | 1 | | 1 | | 2 | | | |
| Swansea | | 4 | | | | FAME | | | 20+ | 4 |
| Wrexham | 2 | 2 | | | | | | | | |
| **Scotland** | | | | | | | | | | |
| Dundee Central | | 3 | | | | | E | E | 10+ | 4 |
| Edinburgh Central | 4 | 2 | | | | | E | E | 5+ | |
| Glasgow Mitchell | 2 | 1 | 1 | 1 | | 1+ FAME | 2 | E | 30+ | 2 |
| **Northern Ireland** | | | | | | | | | | |
| Belfast Central | 2 | 1 | 2 | | | 1+ FAME | 1 | 1 | 1+ | 4 |
| Londonderry Central | | 4 | | | 3 | | | 1 | 1 | 4 |

# Library name, address, telephone and fax number

Aberystwyth Public Library, Corporation Street, Aberystwyth, Ceredigion SY23 2BU, tel 01970 617464, fax 01970 625059

Barnsley Central Library, Shambles Street, Barnsley, S. Yorks S70 2JF, tel 01226 773911, fax 01226 773955

Bath Central Library, The Podium, Northgate Street, Bath BA1 5AN, tel 01225 428144, fax 01225 331839

Bedford Central Library, Harpur Street, Bedford MK40 1PG, tel 01234 350931, fax 01234 342163

Belfast Central Library, Royal Avenue, Belfast, Northern Ireland BT1 1EA, tel 01232 243233, fax 01232 332819

Birmingham Central Business Library, Chamberlain Square, Birmingham B3 3HO, tel 0121 235 4511, fax 0121 235 4458

Bournemouth: Landsdowne Library, Meyrick Road, Bournemouth, Dorset BH1 3DJ, tel 01202 454616, fax 01202 454620

Bradford Central Library (Business & Commerce), Prince's Way, Bradford, W. Yorks BD1 1NN, tel 01274 753656, fax 01274 753687, Email christine.dyson@bradford.gov.uk

Bristol, Library of Commerce, Bristol Central Library, College Green, Bristol BS1 5TL, tel 0117 927 6121, fax 0117 922 1081

Cambridge: Reference and Information Service, 7 Lion Yard, Cambridge CB2 3QD, tel Cambridge 65252, fax Cambridge 62786

Cardiff Central Library, Frederick Street, Cardiff CF10 4DU, tel 01222 382 116, fax 01222 238 642

Carlisle Library, 11 Globe Lane, Carlisle CA3 8NX, tel 01228 607 310, fax 01228 607333

Chelmsford Library (Business Information Service), PO Box 882, County Hall, Chelmsford CM1 1LH, tel 01245 492535, fax 01245 492536

Cheltenham Reference Library, Clarence Street, Cheltenham GL50 3JT, tel 01242 582269

Chester Library, Northgate Street, Chester CH1 2EF, tel 01244 312935, fax 01244 315534

City Business Library, 1 Brewer's Hall Garden, London EC2V 5BX, tel 020 7638 8215, fax 020 7332 1847

Colchester Central Library, Trinity Square, Colchester, Essex
CO1 1JB, tel 01206 562243, fax 01206 562413

Croydon Central Library, Katharine Street, Croydon CR9 1ET,
tel 020 8760 5400, fax 020 8253 1004

Derby Central Library, The Wardwick, Derby DE1 1HS, tel 01332 255 398,
fax 01332 369570

Dundee Central Library, The Wellgate, Dundee DD1 1DB,
tel 01382 434 025, fax 01382 434 643

Durham City Library, South Street, Durham DH1 4QS, tel 0191 386 4411,
fax 0191 384 1336

Edinburgh, The Reference Department, Central Library, George IV Bridge,
Edinburgh EH1 1EG, tel 0131 225 5584, fax 0131 225 8783

Ellesmere Port Library, Central Reference and Information Service, Civic
Way, Ellesmere Port L65 0BG, tel 0151 355 2286, fax 0151 355 6849

Exeter Central Library, Castle Street, Exeter, Devon EX4 3PQ,
tel 01392 384 206, fax 01392 384 316

Glasgow, The Mitchell Library, North Street, Glasgow G3 7DN,
tel 0141 287 2901/2/3/4, fax 0141 287 2815

Hartlepool Central Library, 124 York Road, Hartlepool, Cleveland TS26 9DE,
tel 01429 272 905, fax 01429 275 685

Hatfield, Central Resources Library, New Barnfield, Traveller's Lane,
Hatfield, Herts AL10 8XG, tel 01707 2815, fax 01707 281514

Hull Central Library, Albion Street, Kingston upon Hull, HU1 3TF, tel 01482
883083, fax 01482 883080

Leeds Central Library, Information for Business, Calverley Street, Leeds LS1
3AB, tel 0113 247 8265, fax 0113 247 8268

Leicester Reference & Information Library, Bishop Street, Leics LE1 6AA, tel
0116 255 6699, fax 0116 255 5435

Liverpool Central Libraries, William Brown Street, Liverpool L3 8EW, tel
0151 225 5429, fax 0151 207 1342

London, Science Reference Library, British Library, Southampton Buildings,
London WC2A 1AW, tel 020 7412 7494

Londonderry Central Library, Foyle Street, Londonderry, Northern Ireland BT48 1AL, tel 01504 266888, fax 01504 269084

Manchester Central Library, Commercial Library, St Peter's Square, Manchester M2 5PD, tel 0161 234 1990, fax 0161 234 1963

Middlesbrough Central Library (Marketing Information Centre)Victoria Square, Middlesbrough TS1 2AY, fax 01642 648077

National Library of Wales, Aberystwyth, Ceredigion, SY23 3BU, tel 01970 623801, fax 01970 632882

Newcastle City Library, Princess Square, Newcastle upon Tyne, NE99 1DX, tel 0191 2610691, fax 0191 2611435

Newport: Office for National Statistics Library, Room 1001, Government Buildings, Cardiff Road, Newport, NP9 1XG, tel 01633 265539, fax 01633 222615

Norwich Information Library, Gildengate House, Anglia Square, Upper Green Lane, Norwich NR3 1AX, tel 01603 215251 (no fax)

Oxford Central Library, Westgate, Oxford OX1 1DJ, tel 01865 810191, fax 01865 721694

Reading Business Library, Central Library, Abbey Square, Reading RG1 3BQ, tel 0118 950 9245

Southampton Business Library (part of the City Library), Civic Centre, Southampton SO14 7LW, tel 01703 832958, fax 01703 336305

Swansea Reference Library, Alexandra Road, Swansea SA1 5DX, tel 01792 516753, fax 01792 636235

Truro Business Information Unit, Cornwall Reference Library, Cornwall County Library, Union Place, Truro, Cornwall TR1 1GP, tel 01872 72702, fax 01872 223772

Winchester Reference Library, 81 North Walls, Winchester, Hants SO23 8BY, tel 01962 846 057, fax 01962 856615

Worcester County Library, Spetchley Road, Worcester WR5 2NP, tel 01905 766 237, fax 01905 766244

Wrexham Library, Rhosddu Road, Wrexham LL11 1AU, tel 01978 927442, fax 01978 292633

# The Office for National Statistics (ONS) Libraries

Based in Newport (Gwent) and London, both the ONS libraries contain virtually every statistic produced by government departments. They also have equivalent economic and population statistics from most other countries of the world. This may be helpful for projects focusing on export market potential.

## Office for National Statistics Libraries

London: 1 Drummond Gate, London SW1V 2QQ (just by Pimlico tube station), tel 020 7533 6363

Newport: Government Buildings, Cardiff Road, Newport, Gwent NP9 1XG, tel 01633 812973

The ONS libraries hold two sources of business data which are rarely seen elsewhere: *Sector Reviews* and *Consumer Trends*. Both are very useful, especially the latter.

## Sector Reviews

These are quarterly analyses of data within sub sectors of the economy. For example the *Food, Drink and Tobacco* volume provides data on production, exports, employment, wages, capital expenditure and value added. This is broken down into individual markets such as for pet foods, wine, soup and cider. Further tables break the information down even more, so that you could find out that, of 55 wine producers in Britain, nearly half have annual turnovers below £50,000. This is great if you are doing a project on setting up an English vineyard, for example.

*Sector Reviews* cover: food, drink and tobacco; textiles; metals and metal products; paper, publishing and printing; machinery and domestic appliances; vehicles and other transport; wood products and furniture; electrical and electronic equipment.

## Consumer Trends

This quarterly volume provides some exceptionally useful information on consumer markets. The data is broken down very finely (e.g. there is a category for driving lessons) and therefore provides useful information on market size. The data is also given quarterly, so seasonal patterns of demand become clear (very useful for cash flow forecasting). Trends in the data are also clear and can be used to extrapolate for sales forecasting.

## Other useful publications

The following are produced by the Office for National Statistics (available at most libraries):

*Annual Abstract of Statistics*: a marvellous resource for past data; to enable comparisons to be made between now and a decade ago. You might for example want to look at car ownership today compared with ten years back, to set into a context a rise in the turnover of a garage.

*Economic Trends* contains all the main economic indicators, including GDP, inflation, employment and unemployment, production and interest rates.

*Labour Market Trends* is a very detailed source of information on wage rates and prices, broken down into small subsectors. If you want to know the wages and working hours of sea fishermen, this is the place. It also gives detailed information on the rate of training within the UK labour market.

*Monthly Digest of Statistics*: the best source of up to date information on population, inflation, production, employment, investment and the weather.

*Social Trends* is an annual publication which has useful data about people's lives. If you wanted to know what proportion of households own a dishwasher or a CD player, this would be the volume to look in. It is also good on people's leisure habits, such as cinema going or the number who play particular sports.

## 4 Books for tackling specific project objectives

The list that follows provides detailed references to some of the many books on starting and managing small to medium-sized firms. There are so many possible project topics that this section can only provide a hint of what is available.

| Project Focus | Title and Author | Publisher and Publication date | ISBN |
|---|---|---|---|
| **Business start-ups – general** | | | |
| Starting up | *Lloyds Bank Small Business Guide 1998*, Williams S. | Penguin, 1998 | 0 1402 6836 7 |
| | *101 Ways To Start Up Your Own Business*, 2nd Ed, Ingham C. | Kogan Page, 1997 | 0 7494 2186 X |
| | *Starting Up*, Jones G. | Pitman, 1995 | 0 273 61701 X |
| Business planning | *24 Hour Business Plan*, Johnson R. | Century Business, 1997 | 0 7126 7779 8 |
| | *How To Prepare a Business Plan*, Record M. | How To Books, 1995 | 1 85703 178 4 |
| Franchising | *Daily Telegraph Guide To Taking Up a Franchise*, Barrow and Golzen | Kogan Page, 1998 | 0 7494 1836 2 |
| **Business start-ups – specific** | | | |
| Starting/running a pub | *The Publican's Handbook*, Bruning T. | Kogan Page, 1997 | 0 7494 2296 3 |
| | *Running Your Own Pub*, Money E. | Kogan Page, 1994 | 0 7494 0667 4 |
| Starting/running a catering business | *How To Open and Run a Successful Restaurant*, 2nd Ed, Egerton-Thomas C. | Wiley, 1995 | 0 471 04236 6 |
| | *Start and Run a Profitable Coffee Bar*, Metzen & Harrison | Self Counsel Press, 1997 | 1 55180 098 5 |
| Starting a travel agency | *Travel Agency Practice*, Horner P. | Longman, 1996 | 0 582 28856 8 |

A
B
C
D
E
F
G
H
I
J
K
L
M
N
O
P
Q
R
S
T
U
V
W
X
Y
Z

**Other business issues**

| Selling a business | *How To Sell Your Business*, Ziman R. | How To Books, 1994 | 1 85703 119 9 |
| Business expansion | *Business Growth Action Kit*, Brown J. | Kogan Page, 1997 | 0 7494 1795 1 |
| Marketing for a small firm | *Teach Yourself Marketing Your Small Business*, Jay R. | Hodder & Stoughton, 1996 | 0 340 65474 0 |
| | *Successful Mail Order Marketing*, Bruce I. | How To Books, 1996 | 1 85703 334 5 |
| Cash flow management | *Managing Credit*, Hedges R. | How To Books, 1997 | 1 85703 373 6 |
| | *Managing Budgets and Cash Flows*, 2nd Ed, Taylor P. | How To Books, 1996 | 1 85703 344 2 |
| Business on the Internet | *Understanding Business On The Internet*, 2nd Ed, Norton & Smith | Hodder & Stoughton, 1998 | 0 340 70540 X |
| | *Successful Web Sites*, Morris & Dickinson | Hodder & Stoughton, 1998 | 0 340 70508 6 |

## 5 Organisations which may be helpful in project research

## A–Z of Sources of Information for Projects and Assignments

| Name, address and telephone number | Type of information obtainable |
| --- | --- |
| *Advertising, Institute of Practitioners in* 44 Belgrave Square, London SW1X 8QS, tel 020 7235 7020 | The source of information on advertising methods and effectiveness; good library on advertising, but not a public library; write/call only when you are clear about the information you need. |

*Advertising Standards Authority (ASA)*
Brook House
2/16 Torrington Place,
London WC1E 7HN,
tel 020 7580 5555

May be useful on the role of the ASA in policing advertising standards.

*Advisory, Conciliation and Arbitration Service (ACAS)*
180 Borough High Street,
London SE1 1LW,
tel 020 7210 3613

Can provide figures on trends in unfair dismissals, industrial disputes, the use of pendulum arbitration and much more. The ACAS Annual Report contains good data and useful case histories; useful for projects on trades unions or HRM

*British Franchise Association*
Thames View, Newton Road,
Henley-on-Thames,
Oxon RG9 1HG,
tel 01491 578050

Possible starting point for research into a feasibility study; can supply a 'franchise start-up pack', but so can most of the high street banks.

*British Standards Institute (BSI)*
389 Chiswick High Road,
London W4,
tel 020 8996 9000

Can provide details on British Standards, how to achieve the kitemark and how to qualify for BS 5750 or BS 7750. Can provide case study material on success at achieving these awards.

*Central Office of Information*
Hercules Road,
London SE1 7DU,
tel 020 7928 2345

Facts on government policies and government advertising.

*Chambers of Commerce, Association of British*
9 Tufton Street,
London SW1P 3QB,
tel 020 7565 2000

Find the address of your local chamber of commerce; the local branch may help you with local contacts and knowledge.

*Commission for Racial Equality*
Elliot House,
10-12 Allington Street,
London SW1E 5EH,
tel 020 7828 7022

Can provide advice and leaflets on legal requirements and obligations to employees; useful for a project on recruitment, training or appraisal, where discrimination can often creep in.

*Companies House*
21 Bloomsbury Street,
London WC1B 3XD,
tel 029 2038 0801

The accounts of all limited companies are registered here each year; they are obtainable by post or by turning up in person (before 15.00 each weekday).

A B C D E F G H I J K L M N O P Q R S T U V W X Y Z

| | |
|---|---|
| *Companies House*<br>Crown Way,<br>Maindy,<br>Cardiff CF4 3UZ,<br>tel 01222 388588 | The accounts of all limited companies are registered here each year; they are obtainable by post or by turning up in person (before 15.00 each weekday). |
| *Companies House*<br>Birmingham Central Library,<br>Chamberlain Square,<br>Birmingham B3 3HQ,<br>tel 0121 233 9047 | The accounts of all limited companies can be viewed here on the companies house computers. Data can be viewed or printed off. |
| *Companies House*<br>37 Castle Terrace,<br>Edinburgh EH1 2EB,<br>tel 0131 535 5800 | The accounts of all limited companies can be viewed here on the companies house computers. Data can be viewed or printed off. |
| *Companies House*<br>7 West George Street,<br>Glasgow G2 1BQ,<br>tel 0141 221 5513 | The accounts of all limited companies can be viewed here on the companies house computers. Data can be viewed or printed off. |
| *Companies House*<br>25 Queen Street,<br>Leeds LS1 2TW,<br>tel 0113 233 8338 | The accounts of all limited companies can be viewed here on the companies house computers. Data can be viewed or printed off. |
| *Companies House*<br>75 Mosley Street<br>Manchester M2 2HR<br>tel 0161 236 7500 | The accounts of all limited companies can be viewed here on the companies house computers. Data can be viewed or printed off. |
| *Confederation of British Industry (CBI)*<br>Centrepoint<br>103 New Oxford Street,<br>London WC1A 1DU,<br>tel 020 7379 7400 | The CBI publishes many reports on business performance; most useful is the *Quarterly Industrial Trends Survey*. |
| *Consumers' Association*<br>2 Marylebone Road,<br>London NW1 4DF,<br>tel 020 7830 6000 | Publishers of *Which?* magazine, covering many issues in marketing ethics and honesty. |
| *Design Council*<br>34 Bow Street,<br>London WC2,<br>tel 020 7420 5200 | Data and case histories about the importance of design in boosting competitiveness. |

*Equal Opportunities Commission*
Overseas House,
Quay Street,
Manchester M3 3HN,
tel 0161 833 9244

Information and case histories about
the legal obligations of employers.

*European Commission*
Information Office
8 Storey's Gate,
London SW1P 3AT,
tel 020 7973 1992

Information on EU policies
and developments.

*Eurostat Publications*
Office of Official Publications
of the European Union
PO Box 276,
London SW8 5DT,
tel 020 7873 0011 (24 hours)

Publications providing statistics on
the European Union.

*Health and Safety Executive*
2 Southwark Bridge
London SE1,
tel 020 7717 6000

Workings of the Health and Safety Act,
the Health and Safety Executive and
COSHH regulations; useful source of
information on safety for a project
on a new work system or equipment.

*Industrial Society*
48 Bryanston Square,
London W1,
tel 020 7479 1000

For unbiased information on human
resource issues such as
employee/employer relations and
performance appraisal.

*Institute of Management*
Third Floor,
2 Savoy Court,
Strand,
London WC2R 0EZ,
tel 020 7497 0580

Analyses of the workplace performance
of business; many publications produced
each year on management issues.

*Institute of Personnel and
Development (IPD)*
IPD House, 35 Camp Road,
London SW19 4UX,
tel 020 8971 9000

Informative library for human
resource and workplace performance
issues; library may be willing to help
answer very specific queries (such as
'What's the national average for labour
turnover?').

*Investors in People (IIP)*
7 Chandos Street
London W1
tel 020 7467 1900

Head office for the organisation that
accredits firms' efforts to achieve the
IIP standard.

A
B
C
D
E
F
G
H
I
J
K
L
M
N
O
P
Q
R
S
T
U
V
W
X
Y
Z

*Market Research Society*
15 Northburgh Street,
London EC1V OAH,
tel 020 7490 4911

Provides information on market research methods, a list of market research companies and case histories on the value of market research.

*Office for National Statistics*
The Stationery Office
PO Box 276,
London SW8 5DT,
tel enquiries (24 hours):
0870 600 5522

The publishers of a wide range of government statistics, including volumes such as the *Annual Abstract of Statistics* and *Economic Trends*.

*Office of Fair Trading (OFT)*
15–25 Bream's Buildings,
London EC4A 1PR,
tel 020 7211 8000

A good way to find out if there has been an OFT report into the business you are looking at (most likely if there is some element of monopoly in the marketplace); OFT reports are a data goldmine.

*Small Firms Service*
Department of Trade and Industry
Kingsgate House,
66–74 Victoria Street,
London SW1E 6SW,
tel 020 7215 5000

Good starting point for information on government policy towards, and assistance to, new small firms.

*Society of Motor Manufacturers and Traders*
Forbes House,
Halkin Street,
London SW1X 7DS,
tel 020 7235 7000

The suppliers of monthly data on car and truck sales providing figures on market size, brand and sector shares and giving good scope for analysis of seasonality and trends.

*Stock Exchange*
Old Broad Street,
London EC2N 1HP,
tel 020 7588 2355

Useful leaflets on sources of finance for public limited companies.

*Trades Union Congress*
Congress House
Great Russell Street,
London WC1B 3LS,
tel 020 7636 4030

Projects benefit from a wide range of views; why not see if the trades unions have anything to say on performance appraisal, training or any other human resource issue?

## 6 Other sources of data

| Source | Type of data available |
|---|---|
| *CBI Quarterly Industrial Trends Survey* is the Confederation of British Industry's quarterly survey into business confidence. | Available in larger libraries; alternatively you could try CBI, Centre Point, 103 New Oxford St., London WC1A 1DU. |
| Chambers of Commerce are voluntary associations of local businesspeople. They might be invaluable sources of information and contacts for project work (but some are helpful, others less so). | All contact details are in *Trade Associations and Professional Bodies in the United Kingdom*, published by Millard and regularly updated. At the time of writing, the 12th edition is current. |
| Up-to-date government economic data are often important, both to provide background understanding and as a way of analysing company information. | The main sources of information are the *Monthly Digest of Statistics* and *Economic Trends* (also monthly). For the very latest data, look at the last week's copies of the *Financial Times*. The contents table on the front page will tell you whether it contains the latest economic indicators. |
| *Financial Times CD ROM*: an invaluable way to obtain up to date data about business stories and markets. | Widely available at college and public libraries. |
| Libraries: to see if there is a relevant specialist library or to find the nearest main library use *Libraries in the UK* published annually by the Library Association Publishing. | A wide variety of information; if in doubt consult the librarian; it is what they are there for. |
| Office for National Statistics Library: vast resources in UK and international business and economic statistics. Open 9.00–5.00 Monday–Friday. | 1 Drummond Gate, London SW1V 2QQ, tel 020 7533 6363, fax 020 7533 6261, or Government Buildings, Cardiff ` Road, Newport, Gwent NP9 1XG, tel 01633 812973, fax 01633 812599. |

A
B
C
D
E
F
G
H
I
J
K
L
M
N
O
P
Q
R
S
T
U
V
W
X
Y
Z

Trade associations to find whether there is a relevant association, perhaps with library facilities.

*Trade Associations and Professional Bodies in the United Kingdom*, published by Millard and regularly updated. At the time of writing, the 12th Edition is current. This reference book is available at all reference and most public libraries.

Weather, e.g. daily temperature during a month to correlate with sales figures.

National Meteorological Library and Archives, Met Office, London Road, Bracknell, Berks RG12 2SZ, tel 01344 854841

# Appendix

## Examples of good project questionnaires

1   This questionnaire was written by Clare Pomroy as part of a project titled 'Can John Innes Tennis Club reverse the decline in membership through diversification?' By the time of carrying out the survey she had already identified that opening a gym was the only plausible option for the club. The research objective was to measure the likely uptake by members.

   The following was a self-completion questionnaire, so Clare took care to give clear instructions on how the members should fill it in. The questionnaires were left in a box at reception and returned there when completed.

2   This questionnaire was part of Claire Marston's project into crowd attendance at Fulham Football Club. Her postal survey of football clubs proved surprisingly effective. The following questionnaire was addressed to the Commercial Director of various football league clubs. It was mailed together with a self-addressed (but not stamped) envelope. She had anticipated a response rate of 20%, but the actual response rate was 70%! Note that it is very quick and easy to fill in; also notice that she forgot to include a space for the clubs to identify themselves!

## QUESTIONNAIRE 1

**A Questionnaire for Club Members**

My name is Clare Pomroy, member 243. Could you please spare a moment to help me in the research for my A Level Business Studies project? Please fill out this questionnaire and leave it in the box provided. Could I urge you to do it now, rather than take it away, because a high response rate is needed to make the survey valid.

1. How long have you been a member of this Club? _____ months/years

2. Which of the following Club facilities do you use?

| | At least once a week | At least monthly | Less often |
|---|---|---|---|
| Tennis courts | ❑ | ❑ | ❑ |
| Tennis coaching | ❑ | ❑ | ❑ |
| Squash | ❑ | ❑ | ❑ |
| Bar | ❑ | ❑ | ❑ |

3. Over the past few years, has the Club experienced any significant changes:

   Why do you say that?

   For the better _____ _____

   For the worse _____ _____

4. If the Club introduced the following facilities, how often would you use each one?

| | Daily | At least once a week | At least monthly | Less often |
|---|---|---|---|---|
| Weekend dinner/dance | ❑ | ❑ | ❑ | ❑ |
| Snooker | ❑ | ❑ | ❑ | ❑ |
| Fully equipped gym | ❑ | ❑ | ❑ | ❑ |

5. Do you have any non-member friends who might join the Club if it had a fully equipped gym?

| | Please tick | How many? |
|---|---|---|
| Yes, definitely | ❑ | _____ friend/s |
| Yes, very probably | ❑ | _____ friend/s |
| Yes, possibly | ❑ | _____ friend/s |
| Not likely | ❑ | |

6. Are you: Male ❑ Female ❑ Under 30 ❑ 31–49 ❑ 50+ ❑

Thank you for your help. Please put in the box straight away.

# QUESTIONNAIRE 2

To the Commercial Director,

I am an A-Level student in Maths and Business Studies working on a project with Fulham F.C. I am trying to find the 'perfect' mathematical formula to forecast crowd attendances. I would be grateful if you could fill in the questionnaire below and send it back in the enclosed envelope. If any of the questions cannot be answered please leave them blank and send back what you can. *Please* reply, as a high response rate is crucial.

1. Do you have a method for forecasting home attendances?

   Yes ❏          No ❏

2. If so, is it usually accurate to the nearest:

   | 0–500 ❏ | 500–1000 ❏ | 1000–1500 ❏ |
   |---|---|---|
   | 1500–2000 ❏ | 2000–3000 ❏ | 3000+ ❏ |

3. Which, if any of these forecasting methods do you use:

   Based on the same fixture last season     ❏
   Using a computer model     ❏
   A guesstimate     ❏
   Other, please state     ❏

   . . . . . . . . . . . . . . . . . . . . . . . . . . . . . . . . . . . . . . . . . . . . . . . . . . . . . . . . . . . . . . . . .

   . . . . . . . . . . . . . . . . . . . . . . . . . . . . . . . . . . . . . . . . . . . . . . . . . . . . . . . . . . . . . . . . .

   . . . . . . . . . . . . . . . . . . . . . . . . . . . . . . . . . . . . . . . . . . . . . . . . . . . . . . . . . . . . . . . . .

4. I think the perfect forecasting formula should include:

   The home team's league position     ❏
   The home team's recent form     ❏
   Whether Saturday or midweek     ❏
   Special seasonal factors, e.g. Boxing Day     ❏
   Opposition's league position and average home attendance     ❏
   How far the opposing fans have to travel     ❏
   The weather forecast: wet or dry     ❏

a) Does this approach seem appropriate?

   Yes ❏          No ❏

b) Are each of the above factors relevant? Please put a tick or cross in each of the boxes.

c) Are there any other variables that should be included? Please state

**Many, many thanks. Claire Marston, 22 Bloomfield Road, London E12 5JG**